F

Enjoy!

Vince Musaalo

Through Some
MIRACLE
NOT YET CLEAR TO ME

THE NIGHTMARE of LIVING UNDER the DICTATORSHIP of **IDI AMIN** ...and SURVIVING

Vincent Musaalo

Printed in the United States of America

Second Printing, 2010

ISBN-10: 1453745335; ISBN-13: 9781453745335

book design by

JOURNAL
DESIGN
www.JournalDesign.com

Cover design by Kent Bingham
Photo of Kampala, Uganda by Jonathan Gosier

*I am deeply grateful to Dale Smith, Chris Smith, and Andrew Smith
who provided invaluable assistance in editing and revising this book.*

For my mother, Felicitas Musaalo
And in memory of my father, the late Francis Musaalo

For my loving wife, Freda, and my dear children,
Keegan, Megan, Dylan, and Sebastian

My intention in writing this story is not to provide a complete political history of the country of Uganda. Rather it is my personal story, one that I share with you through first-hand experience. It is a story about a family trying to survive under extremely horrible conditions.

It is surreal to think that many Ugandans indeed survived Idi Amin's regime of blood and terror. Those like me, who survived this debacle, will forever have indelible memories of whizzing bullets that were ubiquitous at the time on Kampala streets, as confused masses jockeyed to find refuge in inconceivable places, hoping to cheat death.

Chapter 1

I WILL NEVER FORGET that fateful evening of January 25th, 1971. I was in the kitchen scrunched over my math homework mother had given me when I heard the huge explosion that shattered our world. The impact was so powerful that it knocked me to the ground where I lay stunned for several minutes. I was terrified, my heart thumping as loudly in my ears as the screams and gunfire outside. I had just managed to stand up when a second wave of mortar blasts knocked me down face-first on the kitchen floor amongst the clattering pots and pans which had been hanging on the ceiling.

Mother burst through the kitchen door, panicked for me and my siblings. She was apprehensive. I could see her face tighten up. As the oldest, by training and instinct, I knew it was my responsibility to do what I could to care and protect them.

"Where are your siblings?" she cried, pulling me from the floor. "We are under attack—find them!!!"

I opened the front door, and immediately caught sight of Martin, just two years old. He was terrified, sobbing, and his hand shook as he reached for mine.

"Where's Patrick?" I asked.

"I don't know," he choked. I heard Patrick's little one-year-old voice crying uncontrollably. He was bleeding profusely from a chair which had fallen and trapped him underneath. I ran to him and pulled him out. Together with Martin, we hurried back to the house where mother began attending to the wound on Patrick's head.

"Close all the windows and curtains," Mother ordered as she bandaged Patrick's head. The windows in the living room were already closed, so I dashed to the bedroom, where I again heard gunshots being fired, as if without any order.

My extreme boyish curiosity got the better of me, and I peeked out of the window. Groups of people who had fled their jobs in Kampala were running as randomly as the bullets fired from the machine guns. Old and young were ducking as they heard the whizzing bullets, while others desperately sought refuge on neighbors' porches or pounded on doors, begging to be let in. I ran frantically into the living room to tell mother what I had seen. But before I could, the door flew open—sending us into greater panic. It was father, a police inspector. He was very nervous and very concerned.

"We were worried," Mother's voice quivered. She rushed to him, clasping his arm. "Francis, what is happening in Kampala? What do you know?"

Father directed his attention towards mother. "The people at work say the Ugandan army has sealed off the Entebbe airport," father answered between gasps for air. "Reports say there are tanks on every street in Kampala." Father asked me to bring the portable radio. "I need to see if Radio Uganda has released any official statement about what's happening. This has to be an attempt by some political faction to overthrow the government."

At 3:45 p.m. a voice boomed from the radio. "Fellow countrymen and well-wishers of Uganda, I address you today at a very important hour in the history of our nation. A short time ago, men of our Armed Forces placed control of Uganda in my hands. I am no politician, but a professional soldier, and therefore a man of few words, and shall be brief. Throughout my professional life, I have emphasized that the military must support a civilian government which has the support of its people, and I have not changed that position."

Such seemingly harmless words, "The military must support a civilian government"—spoken by a general who had just used bullets, mortars and tanks to attack the civilians he now presided over! Thus began the "presidency" of General Idi Amin. With brutal military action, he had wrestled power from unpopular Milton Obote while he was returning from Singapore where he had just attended a Summit of Commonwealth Heads of government. Obote fled to Tanzania and a reward was offered for him—dead or alive.

Amin soon attracted attention on the international scene with his numerous telegrams to the other heads of state. He called Nixon, the U.S. President at the time, "my dear brother," and wished him a quick recovery from the Watergate scandal. He congratulated the Chilean Junta when it assumed power, and even ordered Her Majesty, Queen Elizabeth of England, to send a Scottish guard to accompany him to the commonwealth conference.

Chapter 2

THAT YOUNG BOY running from mortars and bullets, seeing the fear and horror in the face of a mother and children, and seeing his world change with an explosion and radio announcement, but without complete understanding, was me.

My name is Vincent Musaalo, although most of my friends here in the U.S. call me Moose. Because of the problems emanating from the pronunciation of my name, my friends changed my surname Musaalo to Mus; and later to Moose, the American version. I was born in Uganda, a beautiful landlocked country off the East coast of Africa, a country that Winston Churchill once described as the "Pearl of Africa." I was born during the time when most African nations were demanding their independence from the colonial masters who had ruled most of Africa since 1885, the year the African continent was partitioned by the European powers at the Berlin Conference. I have vivid recollections of my family and extended family talking passionately about the aftermath of the Mau-Mau rebellion in my early years. Mau-Mau, *Mzungu Aende Ulaya—Mwafrika Apate Uhuru* was a Swahili slogan that translates in English to "Let the white man go back to Europe; let the African attain freedom."

Although the uprising failed militarily, it may have hastened Kenyan independence. It undoubtedly created a rift between the British colonial community in Kenya and the Home office in London that set the stage for Kenyan independence in 1963.[1]

For several decades prior to the eruption of this conflict, the occupation of land by European settlers was an increasingly bitter point of contention. Most of the land appropriated by the British settlers was in the central highlands of Kenya, which had a cool climate compared to the rest of the country and was inhabited primarily by the Kikuyu tribe. By 1948, 1.25 million Kikuyu were restricted to 2,000 square miles (5,200 km^2), while 30,000 British settlers occupied 12,000 square miles (31,000 km^2).[2] The most desirable agricultural land was arguably in the hands of the colonialists.

A colonialist might possess six thousand acres of land of which one thousand acres were squatters' land, what the Kikuyus called their *shambas*, the Swahili word for "gardens." The squatters held a few acres on a white man's farm and in return had to work for him or her for a certain number of days in the year. When the coffee plantations were harvested, the Kikuyu would load the coffee sacks, twelve to a ton, with sixteen oxen to each wagon, and would start on their way in to Nairobi railway station. The coffee would then be on the ocean in a day or two and sold at the big auction sales in London.

The leader of this revolt against British rule was the famous Jomo Kenyatta…the light of Kenya and of Africa, our motherland. He and the rest of the freedom fighters dealt a staggering blow to British colonial governance in Kenya. Although father was not a Kenyan, and had not participated in the rebellion against British rule there, he was profoundly passionate about its significance to colonial Africa. He was a visionary of Africa's self-determination and a staunch advocate for Pan-Africa, a popular movement then that advocated, among many other

---

1 "Mau Mau Uprising." *New World Encyclopedia*. Web. <http://www.newworldencyclopedia.org/entry/Mau_Mau_Uprising>.

2 Mwakikagile, Godfrey. *Kenya: Identity of a Nation*. 1st ed. Pretoria, South Africa: New Africa, 2007. 26. Print.

things, Africa's liberation from foreign subjugation. It would be years later that I learned of the immensity of the struggle and the thousands of lives that perished in that protracted resistance. In those days independence was not just granted to you. African nations had to fight relentlessly for it. It was tantamount to sacrificing thousands of lives. Even the United States, the mightiest of all nations, was not immune to this type of struggle. The Americans had to fight painstakingly against the British for their freedoms. Through that heavily contested emancipation struggle, the world was again reminded that freedom is a value which must be fought for in every generation.

Father was an Inspector in the Uganda Police and mother taught at Police Children School, a local primary school that catered to the educational needs of the community in which we lived. Mother is a magnificent human being. She remains an attractive, zealous, 5-foot-five woman, although when we were kids, she was plump. She would often say, "Be nice to your friends. It is good to have friends in the neighborhood. If you are nice to your friends, they'll like you." She was also the driving force in our home. If any of us were hit with a bout of malaria, which happened innumerable times, she would run down to the drug store and purchase some quinine tablets. She would grind the tablets, mix them with some herbs, and send us to bed with these orders: "Sleep for ten hours, and sweat it out." I cannot forget the bitter-tasting, colorless drug derived from the bark of certain cinchona trees and used medicinally to treat malaria. Quinine also played a significant role in the colonization of Africa by Europeans. As the precursor of modern pharmacology, quinine was the prime reason Africa ceased to be known as the white man's grave. Some historians have argued that it was quinine's efficacy that gave colonialists fresh opportunities to swarm into East and West Africa.[3, 4]

Because my parents were employed, we enjoyed a relatively modest life. In the late 60's when life's modern amenities and conveniences, such as television and radiograms, were in vogue and infiltrating the African continent, father was able to save up some money and purchase a Sanyo television. I remember with poignant memories watching America's then popular shows which, among others, included *Bonanza, I Love Lucy, Mannix, Batman,* and *Mission Impossible.* In my six-year-old mind I thought all Americans were cowboys, superheroes or world-savers. I didn't understand a word of what the actors said because they did not translate the shows into our native languages. However, it was not the words that captured my innermost interest, but rather the action scenes which caused me to block out everything else common to seven-year-olds around the world, even to this day. I knew if I mastered the art of the cowboys, with their gun swings and prancing horses, I would be the most famous kid on the block. My neighborhood friends would think I was immortal just by mimicking these fancy moves.

We lived in Nsambya barracks, in the quarters reserved for inspectors in the Police Force. The barracks was 3 miles away from Kampala, the capital city of Uganda. Ours was a warm and tightly knit neighborhood where most people were Christians and everybody seemed to know one another, including their respective relatives.

As a young boy, one of the greatest enjoyments was when father arrived home with his colleagues in a Police Peugeot, model 404. I remember running to help him carry his briefcase. Before entering the house, I would ask him to turn on the siren so that I could watch the miraculous light. That always

---

3 Conner, Clifford D. *A People's History of Science: Miners, Midwives, and "low Mechanicks"* New York: Nation, 2005. 95-96. Print.

4 Porter, Roy. *The Greatest Benefit to Mankind: a Medical History of Humanity.* 1st ed. New York: W. W. Norton, 1998. 465-66. Print.

intrigued my boyhood fantasies of following in his footsteps as a policeman. Father was a very kind man. He always played with me. When he was home in the evenings, he would hold me on his lap, and would tell me a story or two. Father would sit quietly, letting me play with him as long as I wanted. I enjoyed our wrestling matches, and he always let me win.

Father was handsome. He was five foot ten, slender, but muscular, and often said, "Eat all the food on your plate; you are a blessed child to have it; many children in the country are starving to death." Sometimes he would ask me if I had taken my cod liver oil, a very disgusting nutritional supplement very popular in the early 70's, that I was supposed to take daily and which left an intense and obnoxious odor of fish in my mouth. He would emphasize "Cod liver oil is one of your best sources of Vitamin A." This led me to believe that the word "vitamin" was synonymous with cod liver oil.

Father's humble and adventurous life had begun 32 years prior on a small farm in the small remote village of Bugube, in Mbale district, in the county of Budadiri, located in the eastern region of Uganda, and bordering with the Republic of Kenya in the east. Mbale district covers a total land area of 2,504 square kilometers, and lies approximately between latitudes 0° 45' N; and 0°35' N and longitudes 34° and 34°, 35' E.

The terrain on which father was raised is home to interesting and unique flora and fauna, magnificent waterfalls, enormous caves, scenic peaks, gorges, and hot springs which bubble up at 480 degrees centigrade. A diverse number of animals inhabit the mountains, including bushbuck, antelope, civet, wildcat, and the elusive leopards which roam below. Bush duikers, hyenas, jackals, rock hyrax, buffaloes, and elephants rove between the forest and the moorland, making the most of the rich ecosystem.

Father grew up on a small farm, in these rugged slopes in a small remote village of 500 farmers, raising coffee, beans, maize, onions, banana plantains, sweet potatoes, cassava, and herding cows and goats on land that is occasionally interrupted by a few upland and mountain ridge extensions.

Like many of the villagers, he had been raised in abject poverty. Thirty years earlier, Great Britain had attempted to relieve the strain of poverty in Uganda by initiating an economic program of raising and selling coffee beans to the rest of the world. His father immersed himself wholeheartedly into this economic enterprise and was determined to plant more coffee trees to pay for his son's education. Accordingly, he enrolled him at a Catholic primary school that catered to the educational needs of its congregation. The learning environment of the missionary Catholic schools, while often morally and physically rigid, was far more advanced than the government schools and played a pivotal role in shaping and streamlining its pupils. Father responded with gratitude and hope to his father's sacrifice.

"I will one day make it," he had reiterated on many occasions while talking to his father, with whom he had established a strong bond and who wholeheartedly believed in his son's abilities.

One does not plow a field by turning it in one's mind, and like a pragmatic man or woman who sets his or her goals and resiliently puts forth the requisite effort to achieve them, father was determined to succeed. He was true to his word, and to his father, graduating near the top of his class at the Police Academy. He was now prosperous, but best of all, he was content because he had married well and had beautiful children: Vincent, Annette, Martin and Patrick. Promotions had come his way, but father still maintained a low profile, never allowing his professional success get into his head.

He was fond of testing my courage often, but little did I know my father wasn't just testing me for fun, but maybe a father's God given instinct was behind it for a future time when that courage would really be tested. One day Father came back from work, and as we were visiting my little five-year-old sister, Annet, came screaming into the living room, saying Mukyakaze, a local derelict we were both scared of, was in the neighborhood. Mukyakaze was probably in his mid forties. He had a shabby beard that hung to the middle of his stomach, and wore several shredded shirts over his big belly. He walked with a distinctive swagger, and his grey hair was in dire need of grooming. Over his shoulder he carried a bag that contained various items he had obtained while rummaging through the trashcans. All my little buddies in the neighborhood had each had their own scary encounter with him, probably exaggerated by boyhood imagination more than reality. Mothers knew of the fear that the children had built around this man and used it to scare them into doing their chores, emphasizing that if they didn't, they would bring the bum to the house.

Upon hearing what Annet had said, Father quickly walked out of the living room and passed our neighbors house to where Mukyakaze was standing and started talking to him. The mere fact that father was talking with him sent cold chills through my entire body, but what froze me in my tracks was when I saw him follow my father back to our house. Before they reached the door, I was under my bed. Then I heard father's footsteps enter the bedroom. He must have known where I was hidden. He reached down and grabbed me. I remember beseeching father not to take me, but my pleading was in vain. He had me stand right before this man, but I'd promised myself that I would not make any eye contact. In the interim, I struggled to keep my knees from shaking. I do not remember much of what transpired that night, for my little mind was in such a state of shock. I was told that father gave him some food, and sent him on his way. If father's goal had been to eradicate the fear I had towards this bum, he fell short of this goal. It wasn't until I was older that my fear of Mukyakaze completely subsided.

Chapter 3

B Y THE SUMMER of 1971, key political and government officials had been reported missing. Rumors circulated that Amin was becoming more and more paranoid and had ordered the secret execution—by firing squad and even mass decapitation—of all military leaders who had not supported his coup.

Something sinister led the new government, and our family soon came to fear it. Father heard Ali Towelli, whose office was adjacent to his own, mention his name—more than once.

"Yes, Inspector Francis Musaalo," he had once heard—the voice angry. But the remainder of the conversation was inaudible to Father and of even more concern than his own name.

"Felicitas has to hear this right now. She has to know this," he roared inaudibly, grabbing his car keys. He directed his secretary to reschedule his appointments and told her that he would be out for the rest of the day. Father briskly stalked out of the office, ready to pounce. Trying to keep the semblance of normalcy, he mentioned the incident to my mother, only after we children were asleep. Then he went back to his office the following morning to try to reason the situation out. To all reason, yet against all belief, he was on a death list. He could approach

Ali—he was after all, supposedly a family friend—but that had every potential for disaster.

It was really no mystery. A close friend, from father's own office, had seen his name in Ali Toweli's office, included with other high-ranking government officials on a list directly from President Amin's office, and addressed to Ali. Father's friend had recited some of the other names which included father's dear friends. He had come across the names while looking for a file regarding Justice Department subpoenas and had secretly confided in Father.

Father had seemingly achieved the impossible, having become one of the youngest Inspectors in the Uganda Police. Although this impeccable record had paved his road to success, his enviable accomplishments did not please Ali. After Amin's assumption of power, tensions and the usual post-coup talk of reshuffling had run high. That had all calmed, my father had hoped. However, the list, the disappearances, and his own name spoken venomously over and over could not be ignored.

"There is only one possibility—he is plotting my death. Is there any other reason for his mentioning my name in such a way?" He tried to think calmly—reason things out, find a remedy. But these times were beyond remediation. "I cannot be in danger!" he exhorted, clenching his trembling fists.

"This is beyond belief! I've worked for twenty years to be where I am, to provide a life for my wife and children. My Felicitas, my children; they need me! Who would care for them if I were killed?" Fear and anger had sapped all his reason. Father's accomplishments, his gifts to his family, his very life seemed to be slipping from his control. But he would not react as a coward. He decided to face this trial the way his father had taught him, like a man.

Gracing the wall opposite him was a majestic portrait of his graduation, which seemed to sum up all the obstacles he had endured to achieve his goal of becoming a police officer and police inspector. He walked towards it, carefully unhooked it from the wall, and gazed at it, contemplating through it the arduous journey that had led him to this place and time. Then he rushed home to tell mother what had happened.

"You are home early," mother said hurrying to the door. "Are you okay?"

Mother could tell from my father's disposition and countenance that something was bothering him.

"Francis what's wrong my dear? You are beginning to scare me." Mother's eyes were bulging as she studied the worried expression on father's countenance. "You are ..." she began, but the door flew open, changing the intense atmosphere, and Patrick, who had recognized father's voice, came running in.

"Father," Patrick exclaimed. Father reached down and gave my brother, Patrick, the usual warm hug, and cautiously carried him to avoid his drool.

"Let's talk sometime tonight when the kids go to bed," Father said. "You mean you will stay around tonight?" mother inquired with profound consternation. "This is really strange," she calmly thought to herself. "I can't believe he will not be at the Flamingo bar tonight. Something must be happening. Had he gotten in a fight at work with his boss, or was he fired from his job?" Mother didn't know what to do. She could not conjecture what seemed to trouble Father. She had given up brainstorming and second-guessing. All she had to do was to wait patiently. She was looking forward to the time when Father would open up and share with her what seemed to be ailing his heart. At 9 p.m. all the kids were in bed and could be heard sleeping heavily.

"Well, Felicitas," Father began, "something strange happened at work."

"You didn't get in a fight with your boss, did you?"

"No ... uh ... this is much more serious than that. I feel like my life is under intense scrutiny and that someone is coming after me." Francis looked pensive, and mother was apprehensive.

"Under scrutiny?" mother quickly interjected. She carefully repeated each word Father had used, trying to find a hidden meaning in them.

"Yes, my life is under scrutiny," Father replied, his voice breaking up as he spoke. His eyes began to tear up, and he paused for a minute to regain his composure, and then proceeded. "Remember when I told you about how my colleague at work had seen my name in red ink with several other high ranking officials in a letter from the office of the President in an investigation file?"

"Of course I do," she quickly acknowledged.

"Well, this morning, while at work, I was on my way back from the restroom when I overheard my name mentioned three times by Ali."

"You mean Ali Toweli, our neighbor?"

"Yes, and I eavesdropped. The tone of the conversation was serious. I could tell he was very angry. He's conspiring to do something evil to me. He wants to kill me."

"To kill you?" she repeated. "You must have pulled things out of context." Mother was trying to calm father's emotions. "Ali's wife and I are great friends. As a matter of fact, she brought over some homemade chapatis for me yesterday."

"You don't get the point!" Father replied furiously, but Mother was completely oblivious to all of this. Father tried to simplify the details of his predicament.

"Ali is part of the newly formed special research unit…a repressive spy unit. He's an undercover spy for Idi Amin, the President…. and besides, spies never divulge any confidential information to their wives. Now do you understand, do you?"

Mother was overwhelmed. She immediately collapsed into fear and panic. She was now beginning to understand the magnitude of the dilemma her husband was engulfed in. The rumors she had heard within the community about Ali being linked to the disappearances now seemed credible.

"How could he pretend to be a friend, and yet conspire to plot my husband's death?" Now she hated her association with Ali's wife, and believed Ali was a traitor. "What are we going to do?" she thought. Of course, there was not very much they could do. Attempting to console her husband, she uttered, "It is okay. You've not done anything wrong. They won't hurt you."

This consolation, however, did nothing to curb my father's worries. He could see right through mother's naiveté. Father was cognizant of the catastrophe that loomed over both our household and the once peaceful community. Like dark clouds that slowly gather before a storm, he could feel the change in the political climate. Learned men and businessmen were disappearing. Some families were secretly annihilated, but no one ever dared to openly take a stance on this sensitive issue. No one wanted to put his or her life in harm's way. His achievements didn't matter now. He was in danger. His friends were in danger. His family would be lost too, were he gone.

It was now approaching 1 a.m., and my father could see that mother was getting drowsy and losing her concentration. She had to teach school the following morning, so she rolled over on her side, kissed father goodnight, and immediately retired to bed.

Father tried to sleep, but couldn't reconcile his feelings, realizing that, perhaps, his life was just about to slip away from him. He knew that a conspiracy was well underway. When he left for work the following morning, father was profoundly demoralized. With a shaky hand, he opened his office door, still deep in thought.

"What if Ali comes after me?" He wondered. "I would be a dead man."

Finally, he sighed deeply, acknowledging the realities of terror that surrounded himself, his friends, and his family; yet, able to do nothing. He contemplated fleeing the country, but couldn't even think of one possible way he would escape without his family. They would be perceived as traitors and would be ostracized, or even worse, face death by firing squad. And as if that was not enough, he didn't have relatives, let alone friends in neighboring Kenya or Tanzania. He tried to put this dilemma into perspective as the pieces of this confusing puzzle began to fit together in his mind.

"First of all," he muttered to himself, "Ali's from the President's tribe and also affiliated with the newly formed repressive spy network whose job it is to carry out heinous crimes on behalf of the government. Secondly, Ali has been linked to another abrupt disappearance."

The victim's body had recently been discovered floating on the King's lake located in the suburbs of Kampala. Rumors had it that Ali had orchestrated his death.

These intense thoughts continued to consume his mind through dawn. Shortly thereafter he fell asleep.

Chapter 4

FATHER SET ASIDE thoughts of his danger for the time being to focus on the continuing needs of his family. A year later, when I was seven years old, with the intention of giving me the benefits of a good education, father enrolled me in Mugwanya preparatory school, a boarding school run by the Banakaroli Catholic Brothers located twenty-five miles away from home. Most of the well-to-do Catholics sent their children to this school, hoping to give them a head start in their academic pursuits. It was believed that this prep school was one of the best in the nation, and since it was a private school, it had enough money to sustain its curriculum without depending on government subsidies. My parents had once before talked about sending me to this boarding school, but I was too young to understand what all that meant. I had never left home without mother or father, and in my little mind, I figured I would come home after a couple of days. Then one Sunday evening, mother dressed me up, packed all my earthly belongings, and just like that, I left home for boarding school. My brothers and sisters, my life-long and most cherished playmates were puzzled by my sudden departure, but they were too young to comprehend why all of a sudden I was leaving in such an unceremonious fashion. Our neighbor's son, Henry Mudumba was heading out to the same school, and his father volunteered to drive us there.

I do not recall a lot about our journey, as I was overwhelmed by the notion of leaving home. However, I remember sobbing when I finally discovered for the first time mother was leaving me in the hands of these unfamiliar, strange-looking men dressed in white cassocks. I don't know how long I continued the crying. I only remember it as the saddest day of my life. I was later introduced to my classmates, but at such a young age, what mattered to me more than anything else was my family; my mother. It was hard this early in life to manage and to complete all that was expected of me in a timely fashion. My former life, friends, family, and routines, were now something I had left at the beginning of that dusty ride in our neighbor's car. Mother had awakened me every morning, bathed me, and prepared breakfast for me and for my siblings. Now it was the harsh and sudden ringing of the dormitory's alarm clock at six in the morning which aroused me from sleep and made me think of my home and family. Instead of mother's bath, and breakfast made with her loving hands, each day was begun with a much harder routine. The school's matron, likely a kind and compassionate woman, but entrenched in her semi-military way of attending to sixty young boys, had her way. I endured, more than relished, her tough baths, scrubbing my small frail body so hard that I felt like I was a plank of wood being sanded and readied for a coat of paint.

We were expected to be in class by eight. Our lessons consisted of Luganda, math, English, Writing, and Physical Education. It was challenging to study in such a rigorous atmosphere at the tender age of 7, and I vehemently resented it. Our teachers were tough, and unrelenting, particularly to the naughty pupils, with whom I was sometimes associated. Visiting days were Saturday and Sunday evenings, my most anticipated days of the week. Because I was too young to remember them, I would pester my teacher each day to find out how many days were left before father and mother would visit me again. I would reiterate this question each day of the week. The thought of visiting day get-ting closer and closer each time I asked helped me to lessen the pangs of homesickness and the longing for the sight and embraces of my family. When that wonderful day would arrive, I would imagine over and over in my mind how wonderful it would be in just a little while longer. Finally, they would show up with the usual, but each time like never before tasted, home-made mandazi, chapati, and somosa treats. Mother would check my entire body to ensure that it was devoid of insect bites, and after visiting with me for about an hour, she would tell me how my siblings at home were doing. The more I learned how my sib-lings were doing, the more nostalgic I felt. Eventually, she would leave, after what seemed to be not nearly a long enough time, and with a stream of tears flowing down my cheeks, I would bid her farewell. It was hard for me to cope with the lonesomeness again, and I would run after the car as they drove away.

At the end of the first term, father picked me up from school. There was such a great anxiety in knowing that I was coming home to see my little brothers and sisters. I was so overjoyed to see them again. No sooner had I settled down than they started telling me all the experiences that had transpired in my absence, like who our new neighbor kids were and who had played with my toys and slept in my bed. They too wanted to hear of my expe-riences at school. I am afraid I made the matron bigger, stronger and tougher than she really was, and the teachers more sullen, strict and stoic than the truth would bear out. It also seemed my stories of school always had the same person as the best soccer player and smartest student.

Then one morning, I was awakened abruptly by mother's frantic voice.

"Wake up Vincent," Mother called, leaning over my bed. But there was no movement. "Vincent, Wake up!" she said again while shaking me.

"Leave me alone," I finally answered as I pushed Mother's arm away. I turned over defiantly, pulling the blanket over my head.

"It's Saturday morning and you always allow me to sleep in," I argued back in an effort to convince her to give me a couple of hours to sleep.

"Son, wake up. Your Father didn't come home last night. Wake up!"

"What... Didn't what?" I mumbled. Although my mind was still fogged by sleep, I could sense desperation in mother's voice.

"I said your Father didn't come home last night." Mother attempted to hide her emotions, but there was still a trembling in her voice. Rubbing my eyes, I sat up in my bed.

"Father didn't do what?"

"He didn't come home."

"Well, maybe he stayed out late with Henry's father. It is not the first time he hasn't come home," I replied, as I tried to talk through a heavy yawn.

"Vincent, some things your mother knows and this is one. I know he didn't stay out late with Henry's father. Things have been happening. Bad things have been happening. Something is not right."

"No," I shook my head. "Go over to Henry's and see. I bet they know where father is."

"You get yourself dressed now. I will be back shortly," mother said as she turned toward the door. Mother left me seated on my bed and rushed across the street to our neighbor's house. As I put my shirt on, I could see the conversation take place between mother and Henry's father. I thought it was peculiar when mother's head dropped, as it appeared that Henry's father didn't know anything about where my father might have been. Before mother returned, I left my room quickly and walked toward my parent's bedroom.

"Father?" I called out naively and waited for an answer. There was only silence. "Father?" more silence.

Gazing upon my parent's bed, I could tell that it was only half slept in. The front door flew open and I spun around to see mother storming through it.

"Henry's father knows nothing! He says they were at the bar earlier last night; however, he left well before your father. Something is wrong." I don't remember ever sensing this heightened sense of worry in my mother.

"Calm down, mother," I said, holding on to my mother's arm trying to muster as much courage, hope and faith as a seven-year-old boy could. "Nothing happened to father. He is a good man. He is an Inspector in the police force. Nobody messes with father. He is just…"

"Just what?" mother interrupted. "Henry's father said they were with friends last night, one of whom was Ali. I don't trust Ali at all. I know something is not right with that man! He must have something to do with father not being here."

"You don't suppose he got hurt do you, like in a fight or something?" I asked with utmost concern.

"I don't know. Maybe I ought to check the hospital." Mother stood thoughtfully for a moment, then quickly turned in my direction. "Hand me my purse," she said with her hand out.

"Do you want me to come too?"

"No, you stay here with your brothers and sister. Don't tell them anything when they wake up." Mother looked at me with one last longing for reassurance. "If anybody could handle himself in a tight situation, it was your father, right?" she asked.

"Father could best anybody in a fight. He's alright," I answered, trying to calm her fears. "That's it; He's down at the hospital. Maybe he's keeping check on people that got in a fight. That's what happened when he didn't come home last night, wasn't it?"

"Yes, I guess he's alright," mother said nodding affirmatively. "Maybe he's down at the hospital." The quiver in my mother's voice indicated that she wasn't convinced. Yet, like all children can do, I overlooked the obvious and was unwilling to think otherwise. I made myself believe that mother would return with good news about my father. After all, father was as good and tough as any of those American TV policemen I liked to watch.

Watching by the window as our car pulled out of the driveway, I caught sight of my mother wiping a tear from her eye. But as I gave it further thought, it wasn't a tear, maybe it was just a speck of dust.

"Henry's father doesn't know anything," I mumbled to myself. "People don't just disappear in the middle of the night! My father is going to be alright, he'll see."

When mother did not find him at the hospital, she embarked on a search, led by her heart, to find father. We had a few relatives who lived around town, plus some family friends. Mother visited them one after another hoping and silently praying the next inquiry would lessen that growing knot in her stomach and burning lump in her throat. None of them had seen him.

It was approaching 2 p.m. on that hot and dusty day in the summer when mother knocked at the door of Aloysius, my mother's younger brother who lived about a mile from our home. She had searched all the bars, nightclubs, and even hospitals, but her effort was in vain. She had spent several hours at the Flamingo bar in particular asking any person who walked through the door if they had seen her husband. She talked to the bar owner, waiters and waitresses, and when necessary, she would show a picture of my father to those who didn't know him. However, this was a tough time to be asking people where and when they had seen my father last, especially for those who knew that he was an inspector in the Police Force. Because of the perpetual rumors that were disseminating across the country about disappearances, no one seemed to be willing to divulge any information to anyone. My mother's closest friends had deserted her. They knew the price they would have to pay if they reported their involvement—sudden death! No one was willing to take the risk.

"I thought I had friends!" Mother agonized. Then she remembered many years ago the invaluable lesson her grandmother had once shared with her. She said, "True friends stand by one another during tough times; they endure hardships together."

However, now mother felt very much alone, in spite of the many friends she had developed and nurtured over the years. She felt the apathy and lack of trust; she was lonesome. The more she thought about her ordeal, the more she missed the company of her true friend and husband—Francis.

My father was very close to Uncle Aloysius, and often stopped by to visit with him. As Uncle Aloysius slowly opened the door, he peeped through the crack and saw that it was my mother.

"This is an unusual visit," he thought to himself, before he ushered her in.

"Come in, Felicitas, come in. Please take a seat," he beckoned, as he cleaned up the couch that was cluttered with newspapers.

"My place is messy," he commented, expecting mother to jump right into the conversation to add a remark or two. But mother didn't say a word. Her face was soaked in tears.

"Felicitas, are you okay? What's wrong…are you guys okay at home?" Uncle Aloysius asked, noticing something peculiar in her temperament.

"I've been looking for Francis since 7 a.m. …and I'm very worried."

"Why…You mean, he didn't come home last night?" Aloysius inquired.

"No," she replied, constantly blinking to clean her eyes of the tears flowing down her face. "He always phones me whenever he finds out he will not come home…this is unlike him. Something is terribly wrong," she managed to respond back as she continued to sob.

Uncle Aloysius desperately tried to console her, but didn't seem to have much success. Minutes later, my Aunt walked through the door and saw my mother crying. She immediately knew something was up. "What's going on?" she inquired as she walked closer to my mother. Mother tried to respond, but was tongue-tied. Realizing that she was unable to articulate her dilemma, uncle, Aloysius, interjected and quickly brought my aunt up to speed.

"Francis is missing, and Felicitas does not know of his whereabouts. She stopped by here to find out if we had seen or communicated with him within the past twenty-four hours." Chills ran through my Aunt's entire body when she heard this.

After a few minutes, mother regained her composure and began unfolding to them the source of her major frustration, recounting the conversation father had previously discussed with her about Ali.

My uncle and my aunt were flabbergasted when they learned that Ali was the prime suspect in my father's disappearance. Although there was no substantial evidence that linked Ali directly to my father's disappearance, Uncle Aloysius was absolutely sure Ali knew his whereabouts. He had heard rumors at work about how Ali had masterminded the death of another inspector. He was furious! He thought about confronting Ali. Uncle Aloysius was very tall and broad, and his deep eyes and thick eyebrows gave him a severe look whenever he was vexed. When his adrenaline was running high, his nerves and muscles stood out on his arms, his back, and on his thighs. He desperately needed an answer from him, but he dropped that idea quickly when he realized the repercussions that might ensue. At least for now, he was not ready to assume that risk.

"Ali is a coward ... He's a murderer!" he growled. When Uncle Aloysius was angry, and could not get his words out quickly enough, he would kick the dirt. Now he wanted to pounce on Ali.

Mother excused herself and got up to leave. But before she departed, Uncle Aloysius arranged to meet her at our home the following day so they could search for my father together. I took up watch by the window, eagerly awaiting the return of mother and father. A subtle disappointment set in when mother walked up to the door without him.

I could tell that the day's humidity had taken a good toll on her. But I also saw how worry, grief and fear about the person you love the most can impact your body and mind more than any external element. She was fatigued, and frozen with fear.

And although we were happy to be reunited, it was difficult not to have father there. The void of father was so noticeable and seemed so real. Undoubtedly, mother must have left no stone unturned in finding father. Mother was scared and, because she was scared, we were scared. I had never seen my family this sad, and young as I was, but still the oldest, I couldn't think of even one possible way of overcoming this melancholic atmosphere that hung over our family.

My heart sunk. Yet like most children my age, I was still optimistic and strongly believed that my father would come home soon.

"Mummy where is Father?" Patrick asked when mother picked him up to comfort him. Mother didn't respond. She just didn't know what to say. "Where is Father?" little Patrick inquired again as he caressed his mother. Mother just didn't know what to tell her son. She attempted to respond, only to be interrupted by her tears, which she desperately tried to hold back with her handkerchief.

"Will Father bring me some bread when he returns home?" Patrick always looked forward to small treats or surprises that my father often brought with him from work. This question, however, was psychologically more mind-boggling than the former and sent my mother into a deep emotional trauma.

"How can I explain to my two-year-old son what has befallen the family?" Mother thought as she continued to cuddle her son. "Children do not comprehend the complexity of the situation! How can a two year old discern our ordeal?" Mother began to think out loud as the emotions in her grew.

"Why has my husband been targeted? Why me? Why us?" The more she questioned our dire situation, the more outraged she became. She was on the verge of losing her mind. She began kicking anything that lay within her reach. Seeing his mother in such a somber mood, little Patrick was scared and began to cry as well, so mother rocked him to sleep and put him to bed.

Mother hurried everyone off to bed and began preparing for bed herself. She had a long day ahead of her, and her plan was to wake early the next day to continue the search of Francis. She was tired and her body was sore, but to make matters even more difficult, she was five months pregnant and still battling morning sickness.

As she prepared to go to bed, her mind was taken back to October 1962 when the dream of Uganda's independence from Great Britain came to fruition. Everybody was happy, and the future seemed bright and promising. She was attending a Teachers Training College, and couldn't wait to graduate and render her long cherished contribution of teaching the future leaders of the country. Schools were cropping up all over Uganda, and she was ready to settle down and go to work. That dream was now fulfilled, and she had been a successful primary teacher for the past twelve years.

However her current trial was quite contrary to the embodiment of *Uhuru*, the Swahili word synonymous with freedom. It was the antidote of that spirit known in former British colonies as self-determination. Less than ten years ago, that spirit of freedom had indeed penetrated the hearts and souls of most Ugandans as it spread across the entire width and breadth of the country.

Finally, two days after father was declared missing, Henry's father, who had joined the search efforts in the suburbs of Kampala, confirmed to my exhausted mother that my father's body had been located floating on a nearby lake. The worry she showed before now exploded draining her of all energy. Her body sagged and she looked about to topple over, tears bursting from her eyes. She was still sobbing when she arrived at the lake. It was not merely terror that held her but something even more terrible. She shuddered. Words fail to express the peculiar strangeness of that shudder which chilled her through and through. Some dry weeds driven by the wind blew rapidly past and appeared to flee with dismay as though pursued. Above her head, the sky was covered with vast black clouds like sheets of smoke. She was profoundly disturbed with dark inner sadness.

She walked bent forward, her head down like an old woman. My uncle was right next to her, and was quietly weeping. When mother finally raised her head, she saw three armed personnel watching her intently and keeping pace with her with each stride she took. She was scared, but more than anything else she was suspicious. She turned to my uncle to say what was on her mind. But the words dried in her mouth. She could not make much headway and was moving along very slowly. She was worn out physically and emotionally, but gathered all her strength, and began to walk courageously.

All of a sudden, Henry's father pointed to what appeared to be a black bag floating on the lake by the shore and said, "That's it!"

Mother was shaking, and as she continued closer, she thought that perhaps it wasn't her husband at all. Maybe it was someone else. Without being conscious of what they were experiencing, mother and my uncle quickly walked towards the black bag. As they drew close to the bag, they realized that it was half-opened. Mother was scared to look. Her heart was thumping fast, her teeth rattling, and her knees shaking. One could hear her intense and heavy breathing. She felt as though she were seized by demons. She could not raise her eyes. My uncle was not immune to this black enormity of nature. But someone had to do it. So he took the initiative. He gave the body one good glance.

"Oh no, Oh Francis, what have they done?" he sobbed. Father's neck had been slashed and the open wounds on his chest seemed to indicate that he had been knifed.

Mother subconsciously opened her eyes, saw the body, and started wailing. She struggled to comprehend her loss. Henry's father was mourning, and shaking his head, thinking about the enormity of the atrocity. A heavy rock and a big piece of rusted metal tied to the body were floating, unveiling the covert intention of the murderers. Their short-lived objective had been to sink my father's body so no one would ever see him again. But God had intervened and miserably thwarted their devious plan.

"Where is all that noise coming from?" I asked my siblings who were all seated in the living room. None of them moved. They were nervous and sat speechless and motionless as they tried to surmise its origination. Overcome with fear, I instinctively rushed to the living room window. Approaching the house was a large group of people. My mother, who was ahead of the group, was sobbing uncontrollably. My uncle and Henry's father were holding her tightly as though they were restraining her from danger. From her deep voice, I could tell that mother was devastated and in deep agony. Never had I seen my mother so demoralized in spirit.

I opened the door and ran towards mother to find out what had happened, but my mother did not even acknowledge me.

"What is the matter?" I asked. The whole scene began to frighten me as I clung onto mother's dress. My uncle moved close to me. He was silent for a while, and was wiping his tears. He did not know what to say.

"Your Father is dead," he finally answered as he wiped down his tears with his hands.

"What do you mean he's dead? I thought Mummy said he did not come home. Didn't she?" The questions I posed my uncle were intricate and evoked more anger and more tears. He was frustrated. Realistically, when does a man or woman ever take time to explain the scary concept of death to a seven-year-old? My uncle grabbed my hand and made his way through the grieving crowd. He had to generate a simple and wise response. I gazed at my Uncle, waiting for an answer.

"Vincent, father is in heaven."

"Heaven? Where is heaven?"

"That is where great men like your father are called to go."

"Do they come back to visit?"

My uncle paused for a minute, and then reassuringly replied, "Yes, they do."

Uncle Aloysius wished he could substitute this statement with a more believable answer than the one he had just given, at least a simple one that would not confound me. But for the moment, his attempt at explaining such a difficult concept pacified my limited understanding of such a deep doctrine. Within minutes, the crowd had gradually mushroomed to about 300 mourners. They came from all directions wailing and mourning. They came to pay their condolences to their friend, and although most of them had heard the rumor surrounding my father's death, not a single soul in the crowd dared say a word about it.

When mother gradually regained her composure, she was somewhat incoherent. I was in profound shock, and my siblings and I joined mother in agony. A day later, my father's body was brought home. I had never heard or seen death, and it was hard for me to even fathom what it was at this early age. But I remember that father's body had two severe wounds around his chest. I was immediately overcome with fear when I saw them. I literally froze. In my little mind, I could picture my father struggling hard to fend off the bandits, but he was definitely overpowered and did not survive. It must have been a tough way to die. Father's life had ended way before its time.

Later, when I was older and mustered the courage to ask mother about that sad day, she told me that prior to this tragedy, father had been suspicious of Idi Amin and his henchmen. He had on numerous occasions expressed his worries to mother. It turned out that one of father's acquaintances, Ali Towelli, who lived a few blocks away, and who was desperate for my father's position, had conspired against my father and had orchestrated his death. He was from Idi Amin's tribe and played a key role in Amin's infamous state research bureau, an underground movement that targeted the elite Ugandans. Idi Amin promoted Ali first to the rank of Inspector, and later on to the post of Commissioner, the highest position in the Uganda Police.

Chapter 5

WE WERE NOT the only family that went through the ordeal of losing a loved one. Many of my mother's friends had lost their husbands as well. At that time, Uganda was going through a political upheaval. Idi Amin, who had just overthrown the government, had ushered in a totalitarian regime and had designed a repressive agenda to eliminate all the high-ranking officials whom he thought might question his policies or overthrow his regime.

The abrupt death of the Chief Justice, for instance, astonished Ugandans who were still oblivious to Amin's secret combinations. Ugandans, including the international community, wondered why Amin would kill a man who was the first prime minister of Uganda.

When Amin took over, on January 25, 1971, he immediately set free Benedicto Kiwanuka, a reputable lawyer and Democratic Party leader who had been detained by Milton Obote as a political prisoner. In 1958, Kiwanuka was elected president general of Uganda's Democraty Party, and three years later won the country's general election and officially became Uganda's first prime minister. It was through his leadership that Uganda gained its independence from Britain on October 9th, 1962. In spite of his initial success, Kiwanuka was later defeated in 1964 by an alliance of Uganda's People's Congress and Kabaka Yekka, Buganda's traditionalist party. This defeat paved the way for Milton Obote to become the country's second leader. Milton Obote, fearing for his life, imprisoned Kiwanuka in 1968, where he remained until Amin ousted Obote two years later.

Kiwanuka was initially impressed by Amin who shook hands with him and who assured him upon his release from prison that his government's first priority was to restore peace, unity, and democracy, and return Uganda to civilian rule as soon as possible. What Kiwanuka didn't understand was Amin was covertly using his popularity to win over Buganda's working class who had rallied behind him in 1964, the year he was declared first prime minister of Uganda.

At a reunion held at his home, Kiwanuka urged all the invited guests to pray to God to give Amin strength and wisdom to complete his mission. Many Ugandans at the time were convinced that Amin would prepare the way for the restoration of human rights, the rule of law and democracy. When the international community was skeptical and resentful about Amin's presidency, Kiwanuka was the first to urge Tanzania, Zambia, and Somalia governments to quickly recognize the legitimacy of the Ugandan government. These countries were harboring anti-Amin elements and providing training cells to the guerilla movements who were determined to overthrow Idi Amin. Kiwanuka was also upset at the isolationist policies of some organization for African Unity member countries which looked down on Uganda's delegation led by Minister Wanume Kibedi in Addis Ababa, on the grounds that Amin's government was illegitimate.

Acting alone, Kiwanuka phoned the Chairman of OAU in Ethiopia and reiterated that Amin enjoyed unanimous support of the people of Uganda. He also warned the council of ministers at the conference not to meddle in the internal affairs of Uganda. In his judgment, Amin was by far a better leader than Milton Obote, the previous president.

Unbeknownst to Kiwanuka, Amin was a silent killer. People were disappearing only to be discovered murdered. As time went on, Kiwanuka became increasingly aware of the wanton killings and atrocities being committed in the entire country. He was disillusioned, considering the fact that he was a lawyer and a staunch believer in human rights.

Amidst all this confusion, Amin phoned Kiwanuka and asked him to become Chief Justice. He grudgingly consented. Although he was a top ranked lawyer, his ambitions resided in politics where he had already created a niche in the late 50's. On June 26, 1971, Kiwanuka accepted his new role as Chief Justice and later sworn in by the Chief Registrar, Mr. K. Kulubya.

In a ceremony following his appointment, Amin stated that no other Ugandan lawyer was better suited for the job to head the judiciary than Kiwanuka. He was confident that Kiwanuka would exercise his functions as Chief Justice in a manner befitting his office as a champion of human rights. Kiwanuka had distinguished himself as a fighter for the defense of the oppressed, both as a politician and as a lawyer. In him, therefore, Amin had a man who understood what oppression meant, and whom the country could trust. The Baganda in particular were ecstatic about his appointment and looked at him as a just and principled advocate who would reform the judicial system which was fraught with corruption.

At the advent of his appointment as Chief Justice, the judiciary was besieged by innumerable problems. In Kampala magistrate courts alone, there were 1800 pending cases. Undue delays with remand cases were common place. The legal services offered were inadequate. Morale had ebbed to unprecedented levels. Judges were apathetic to the concerns of the ordinary people, and the perpetual interference in the administration of justice by Amin's cronies had severely compromised and undermined the integrity of Uganda's judicial system.

Unsatisfied by the glaring weaknesses, the Chief Justice devised a new way of doing things. No sooner had he stepped in his new role than he set out on a national tour of all Ugandan prisons to see firsthand the horrible conditions prevailing in Uganda's prisons. He was shocked by what he saw. He urged the general public to report any judicial malpractice and inconsistencies to the Justice department. He was also told of the gross mistreatment of prisoners, unreasonable denial of bail, and frustrations in the appeals system. He immediately ordered a quick review of bail, remand and appeals cases. He directed that remand should not exceed six months. He also directed that prisoners with petty cases be granted bail without delay. His idea was to speed up the judicial proceedings for he believed that justice delayed is justice denied.

Kiwanuka's priority was to expedite judicial hearings and to remove the enormous bureaucratic bottlenecks which had obstructed the course of justice. In order to ease the workload of the magistrates, he directed that some of the cases be transferred to the high court, which was not as busy as the lower courts. He also tried to boost the morale of the judiciary by improving the terms and conditions of service including enhanced remuneration and perks such as transportation, housing and medical care. He reorganized the judicial system to make it more responsive to the needs of the ordinary people.

On the contrary, Amin was outraged by the Chief Justice's sweeping reforms which he dreaded and resented with utmost fury. How could he fully implement his responsive designs if government blocked his interference in the administration of justice? In his mind, the Chief Justice had committed an enormous crime by indirectly attacking him. Kiwanuka had given himself discretionary powers. Simply stated, the Chief Justice had embarrassed the president.

Within two weeks after that incident, Kiwanuka naively invited the president to attend the silver jubilee of his marriage. Amin did not attend. Amin's reticence should have sent a clear message to the Chief Justice about his deteriorating relationship, but he somehow failed to read the signs.

The Chief Justice's fate was sealed when he sought to uphold the legal rights of one of Amin's victims. Daniel Stewart, a British businessman, was arrested without a warrant and detained at Luzira prison without trial. No judge or lawyer was willing to handle the case. The British High Commissioner in Kampala appealed to Kiwanuka, the Chief Justice, to intervene in the Stewart case and uphold the rule of law. Presumptuously, the Chief Justice agreed to take on the case, despite the fact that he had a hunch that it might present the final duel between himself and the president. Some of his friends advised him to drop the case and flee the country. One of his colleagues concerned for his safety dissuaded him saying, "If the rest of the judges have refrained from handling the case, why don't you drop it too? Just go out of the country quickly, like the rest of the haunted citizens."

However, the Chief Justice had made up his mind. He was determined to handle the Steward case regardless of any repercussions. He told his friends that he would not go into exile because it was his duty to uphold the rule of law and to defend helpless individuals against arrogance and the abuse of power. He knew that running out of the country was no solution to the reign of terror. When he took the weekend off to go visit his friends in his home province, he informed them that he was at loggerheads with Amin in regard to the Stewart case he would be presiding over the following week.

Upon return from his short vacation, the Chief Justice issued a writ of Habeas Corpus Order to Stewart and warned the military authorities about the necessity of observing the laws of the country. He chastised the military stating that they had no power to intervene in the case. Only the police, the law enforcer, had jurisdiction over it. When Stewart appeared, the Chief Justice dismissed the case and ordered the release of the prisoner. Amin was outraged.

Shortly thereafter, the Chief Justice received telephone calls deep in the night. He was already in bed. Then a minister in the office of the president summoned the Chief Justice to immediately report to the parliament building. The Chief Justice was suspicious.

"Why the urgency? If you as a minister want to see me, it is up to you to come to my office. A minister cannot summon a Chief Justice. I will be in the office all day tomorrow."

"But it is the wish of the President."

"The same applies. Come to my office tomorrow."

The following day, no minister showed up at his office. Two days later, the phone rang again. Steven, the Chief Justice's son picked it up. Amin was on the phone. He grabbed it, but Amin hang up. The Chief Justice was suspicious. He instructed his son to sit by it. He waited. After an hour, the phone rang again. A lady secretary told Steven to quickly get a hold of his father.

"Father, it is the President."

The Chief Justice hurried to the phone.

"Who is greater, the Chief Justice or the President?" The Chief Justice did not answer.

"Did you say the government did not have any authority when it arrested Stewart?" Amin continued.

"Yes I did. Legally, soldiers have no right to detain individuals arbitrarily."

Amin was furious. He shouted some expletives, and threw the receiver to the ground. The Chief Justice knew he was in big trouble. His wife, Maxencia, was scared for her husband's life. She hardly slept.

On the 21st of September 1972, after attending Mass at Rubaga Cathedral, he told his wife that he was going to his office. He entered his car and his chauffeur drove him there. As soon as he got to his office, the Chief Justice sat down and pulled out some files. Suddenly, several men in civilian clothes stormed into the office with machine guns. They grabbed the Chief Justice, forced his socks and shoes off and dragged him to a waiting car. They then headed to Makindye, a military police barracks where he was beat up and tortured. Someone at the barracks leaked the story to the media.

The nation was horrified by Kiwanuka's arrest. Every newspaper and radio reported the stunning news, and the inferences drawn from it threw the country into mighty hysteria. The international community condemned this gruesome act and demanded the immediate release of the Chief Justice.

Jomo Kenyata, Africa's sage political leader and President of neighboring Kenya, telephoned Amin and advised him to release the man. The pressure was on.

Amin now realized that he was under intense scrutiny by the international community. He thought of a quick way out. He forged a document alleging that the Chief Justice had been kidnapped by a rebel group based in Tanzania and had been rescued by Amin's security men. Amin's henchmen then presented the forged document to the Chief Justice to sign it. To Amin's bewilderment, the Chief Justice refused.

"I cannot deceive the world and shield the root of our country's evil," the Chief Justice emphasized. The agents were outraged. No living soul in Uganda had ever openly defied Amin.

Amin was irate. He jumped in his black Mercedes, and started the engine. The tires spun out leaving behind a cloud of dust. He drove at breakneck speed, and ran through all the traffic lights. When he arrived at Luzira prison, he was sweating profusely.

"Where is that son of a…? Where is he??"

The prison ward sent for the Chief Justice. He was dragged out of his cell. Amin began interrogating the Chief Justice. Strange noises were heard in the background.

"Don't you know that your life is at my mercy? Don't you know I can kill you?"

"I do," Kiwanuka answered back explicitly. "But I cannot deceive the world. Go ahead and kill me if you like."

Amin's adrenaline was running high. No one has been able to provide a true depiction of the Chief Justice's fate. Some say Amin pulled out a pistol and shot his head several times. Others claim that Amin chopped his head off using a machete and ordered the body to be incinerated.

Next, he ordered his henchmen to kill all the witnesses whose cells were adjacent to Kiwanuka's. Those killed included Kigonya, the Commissioner of Prisons, and a Catholic priest, Father Clement Kiggundu, editor of *Munno*, a popular newspaper which had published the story of the Chief Justice's arrest.

Chapter 6

THE ABRUPT DEATH of the Chief Justice amazed most Ugandans, especially those who were still oblivious to Amin's secret combinations. In some countries, eliminating someone from public office might mean sacking them from their job, or detaining them in a government prison for awhile as the government prosecutors gather evidence relating to the claims or allegations brought against the suspect.

In Uganda, eliminating someone during Amin's regime meant literally killing that person or putting them in prison never to be seen again because he or she "might pose a threat" to the government. Sometimes "show trials" were held to give the appearance of a legitimate and fair system. Most often the evidence against defendants was manufactured and witnesses against them were coerced into giving testimony written by the government. Defense lawyers were useless paid minions of the government, or worse, men who knew their lives and the lives of their families were at risk if they presented too good of a defense.

In order to execute his heinous crimes, Idi Amin created a special repressive spy network, whose job was rounding up and killing all the officers and other elites who had served in the previous regime. Previous government leaders were not the only ones at risk. Intellectuals, scholars, religious leaders, educators, and other people in general who knew the difference between right and wrong, freedom from tyrannical oppression, just seemed to disappear to never be seen again. It was only a matter of time before someone wanting my father's job murdered him."

The aftermath of one man's crime of lust, control, oppression, and the twisted desire to be omnipotent, was so devastating to our family. It instantly and forever changed the life of my family. I did not fully understand what death meant. I thought this tragedy happened only to us. Little did I know then there were hundreds and thousands of little boys like me whose fathers never came home. At that time, I believed it was a temporary departure to some distant place. I must have developed these notions from my little brother, Patrick, who had repeatedly asked mother where father had gone. Out of consolation, mother had reiterated to him that father would come back one day. She too, however, had a hard time dealing with the death and moved out of her bedroom, which she had shared with father, into ours.

As a result of my father's death, our house was taken over by the government. A fortnight later, after my father's funeral, mother received orders from the government to vacate the house immediately. It was then that I came to grips with the emotional trauma that engulfed our family. My home, my family, my friends, and … father gone; all changed in a few moments.

We were lucky to have even found father's body. Many families never buried their loved ones. Sometimes the government would murder a targeted government official and concoct a story about his death. These disappearances were common place, so much so, that women feared for the safety of their husbands, especially when they were late coming home from work. In spite of these worries, many men vanished, never to be seen again, dead or alive. As a direct consequence of these wanton murders, a new and peculiar profession emerged, locally branded as "body finding." Those who benefitted from this beastly endeavor inspired by the devil were again the State Research Bureau Agents. These so-called body finders worked in teams.

When someone disappeared, wives or relatives of the missing person would contact the team and arrange an exorbitant fee for locating the body. These teams were in contact with the murder squads. Sometimes news came directly from the murderers who had connections with the body finders. The fees paid to the body finders were commensurate with the status of the victim. For instance, to track down a missing junior official, the fee was Uganda Shillings 5,000 or USD 600. A senior member in the government would cost the bereaved family Uganda Shillings 25,000 or USD 3,000. Some unlucky families would run into some crooked body finders who would vanish with the money. Often times, the body would be incinerated and an empty coffin would be delivered by Idi Amin's henchmen to the victim's family with special orders from the government not to open it.

These government officials would attend the burial on behalf of the government to express their condolences to the bereaved family. It became a bizarre and twisted business enterprise by men who were "public servants" by day but murderers by night. There were times when an entire family was annihilated.

These were indeed tough and stressful times, and you never knew when your family would have a brush with death. Each knock on the door made each one of us shudder and panic. Many men had been arrested in the presence of their families in broad daylight, flogged, and squeezed into a trunk or back of an army jeep or police vehicle. Some died of suffocation. Some were left out to flounder. Others would be sent to the infamous forest of Namanve, a small village not very far away from the outskirts of Kampala, where they were butchered. It really didn't matter. They were already dead, which was the intent of the capture and arrest anyway. In retrospect, I realize how tragic it was at this early age to be introduced to these heinous killings. This was a trying time to be a Ugandan living in what was once a pleasant and beautiful country. In a short time it became the land of terror, of violence and corruption. It was now a country of people cowering in their homes, trusting no one, not talking, not giving opinion, not growing or progressing; not even enjoying the gifts of God and nature. Ugandans were just surviving for who-knew-how long. They were only hoping that the next day would not be their last. My country's future was bleak and hopeless.

Chapter 7

R AISING A FAMILY under severe circumstances was emotionally draining. "Failure to thrive" is a condition most associated with babies and children not receiving required nutrition to grow. But failure to thrive can also be a result of other absent nutrients. Running, playing, laughing, loving, all these seemed to be withdrawn in my world. And the results were, like the lack of nutrition, often times death. Suicide, alcoholism, and despair so great as to cause irreparable mental illness, all took their toll.

Following father's abrupt death, mother had to find a way of raising our family. She was now about five months pregnant, and with her mind submerged in a sea of endless thoughts, the pain of knowing the unborn child would never have a father and likely grow up in this crazed environment, easily dashed whatever joyful anticipation that accompanies the expected birth of a child. These seemingly unrelenting circumstances must have weighed heavily on mother, leaving her depressed, hopeless, and longing for a way out when no way out was even fathomable. She feared we would be ostracized, or even killed, and knew that our lives were in jeopardy. All of this on top of a mother's basic concerns for her children: food, clothes, education, growing up, marriage and jobs. But she avoided discussing these conspicuous challenges overtly with us. She was somehow able to bring a sense of security to our family during these difficult times.

Mother was born in the early 30's, in a remote village of Nkokonjeru, in Mukono district to loving, strict parents who have since passed on. She was the oldest of five children. Two passed away in infancy. When she was eight, her mother was diagnosed with a mysterious illness, and was admitted to Nkokonjeru Catholic hospital. She was later transferred to Mulago hospital where it was hoped she would get more specialized treatment.

However, grandfather did not come with her because he had spent all his meager income on western and traditional medicine, hoping to find a cure for grandmother's degenerating health. A close relative, who had heard of my grandmother's abrupt illness, gave grandfather some money so he could go visit his ailing wife, but due to some unavoidable circumstances at home, he asked mother to go visit grandmother.

Mother had never been to a big city, but she had no choice. A neighbor helped her catch the bus the following morning, and after a couple of hours, she found herself in Kampala. She had been given directions, but as it turned out, they were wrong. She was stranded and overwhelmed by the hustle and bustle of the city. She was scared of being lost in a city in which she didn't know anybody. She was presumptuous enough to ask a few people how to get to the hospital, but nobody seemed interested in helping her. Finally, a kind man who was sympathetic to her plight volunteered to walk her there. The nurses at the hospital were helpful, but also broke the bad news to her. Her mother was minutes away from dying. They took her to her mother's bed. Her eyes were closed, but when mother grabbed her hand and started talking to her, she immediately opened them for one last time. She recognized mother, closed her eyes, and peacefully passed on.

Twelve miles of walking to school a day does not constitute corporal punishment, but in the early years of my mother's life, it was an enormous burden. It meant that as a seven-year-old girl, she had achieved a remarkable achievement by the simple act of going to school. I believe these walks made her tougher and better prepared for life's challenges. She would wake up at 4:00 a.m. and head out to the family farm to till the land until 6 a.m., when her father would take over so she could prepare for the six-mile journey.

During the rainy season, which lasts between two to three months, the tributaries of Lake Victoria overflow, causing the dust roads to turn into a thick layer of mud buried beneath two to four feet of water. This made it extremely difficult for my mother to get to school.

On a few occasions, she would be chased down by packs of vicious wild dogs, which she describes as running for dear life. It was difficult for mother to get used to these adventures. On many occasions, as I have faced challenges, I have found strength from telling myself, "this is nothing compared to walking to school buried beneath four feet of water and mud, and being chased by wild vicious dogs." These things stay with you, and I know they made my mother stronger. She was no stranger to overcoming trepidation.

When mother woke the following morning, her father was sitting on the edge of her bed. He had something important to tell her, "good morning."

"Good morning father," mother replied. Her voice was still hoarse, her eyes red and swollen, and she was depressed.

"I have something important to tell you," he commenced. Mother listened as she had always done. Her father was a man of few words, and he only spoke when he had something of utmost importance to say.

"Well, Felicitas," he began, as tears rolled down his cheeks, "there are times in life when plans go awry, when anticipated goals fail to materialize, when illnesses or accidents derail the normal flow of daily activity. At such a time, we all need to something to fall back on, inner resources that strengthen our resolve." He then reached out to mother who was buried in tears and hugged her. "Felicitas, the notion of taking one day at a time may seem narrow, particularly when one loses a loved one. When your mother passed away, my heart was torn apart. Josephine was my best friend. We had big dreams, exciting goals for the family. You were barely eight years old. Your two brothers, Andrew and Aloysius, were toddlers. Then one day she was gone. I was devastated. My dreams were shattered. I had to find a way of raising you and your brothers. My sisters offered help. But I could neither relinquish nor relegate that responsibility to anyone, not even to my immediate family. I was determined to work around my new routine and my new lifestyle to accommodate the new changes. Felicitas, you must trust in God and turn to the inner resources that strengthen our resolve. Have faith in him. Felicitas, life may appear to have stopped as we speak, but it has not. Life goes on. Adversity can forge an immature soul into a power-house of strength. You and I will overcome this turbulent time together." He gave mother another hug. This pep talk seemed to revitalize and rekindle mother's spirit who prior to this meeting had looked at life as a thicket of thorns.

At that tender age, I was not oblivious to the challenges we were facing. Life was noticeably different. Life has so many ironies, and we were witnessing a backbreaking ordeal. Money was scarce, and we did not have enough of it to buy food, not even the basic essential commodities. Mother tried her level best to feed us whenever she could, although under such tight economic circumstances, I didn't appreciate how far she managed to stretch a very meager budget. Breakfast was usually simple: left over sweet potatoes, and a cup of sugarless porridge, tea, or coffee.

When mother had a little money to spend, she would purchase half a kilo of sugar on the black market and some powdered milk. On some special holidays, she would fry some mandazi and chapatis. Our mouths would water, as the mandazi and chapatis started to brown in the pan. This was quite a treat; a substantial boost to our breakfast meal.

Mother would prepare lunch at about 12 p.m., and it consisted of a meal of steamed green mashed plantains, called *matooke*, one of the national dishes of Uganda. Mother would wrap the bananas in plantain leaves *endagala* and steam them until tender. She then prepared a delicious complimentary groundnut sauce with mushrooms to go with it. Mother's main meals were centered on a sauce or stew of groundnuts, beans, peas, or Ugandan greens, like *dodo* or *nakati*. She was determined to go without to ensure we got something to eat.

I now longed for the days when father was around. Because of my father's death, my Mother was compelled to find a new school for me and my siblings that was cheaper and within our meager budget. None of father's brothers were educated. Prior to his death, he had supported his father and mother as well as his five elder brothers through his job. On mother's side, her father was always in and out of the hospital, and had consequently given up work on his coffee and banana plantations. With no one left to turn to, mother had to find a quick solution if she were to keep the family together. One of her best friends, also a primary school teacher by profession, came to our rescue by loaning us a tract of land on which to grow a variety of crops to supplement mother's meager salary. This was such a great blessing for our family. Although the work was painstakingly difficult, mother knew that this was the only way available for her to provide for the family's needs.

I consider farming the greatest experience of my life. It kept us from dwelling on the difficulties of our life. We planted all the food we ate, and farming introduced me to manual labor. It also introduced me to the difficult notion of managing a project from inception and seeing it through completion. Unlike the many projects I've been privileged to work on in the corporate world which mostly spanned a couple of months, farming in my family was a year-round activity.

It was excruciating to till the soil in the usual blazing heat and humidity. We planted maize, peas, beans, sweet potatoes, cassava, and banana plantations. Each crop came with unique demands. When we came back home after several hours of uninterrupted work, our hands were replete with calluses, our backs ached, and we were thirsty and hungry. Mother was the last to come home. She would inspect the farm, redo some of our work, and determine the next assignments. She would show up at 2 p.m., and all she ever asked was a cup of water. Her body was worn out.

Although difficult, farming taught me lessons that I've since relied upon in my adult life. Tending crops is not the easiest endeavor, and quite frankly, I don't know how my friends' parents irked out a living during the 1973 economic war, when all the essential commodities were sold on black market. None of them were middle class or privileged. Through this experience, mother taught me to be provident and diligent.

Every morning at six o'clock, after our morning prayer, we all headed out to work. Each one of us was assigned a garden about 40 meters by 40 meters. We each took our piece of land with a profound sense of excitement and urgency for this important stewardship, just like a child who receives a new toy and is determined to protect, guard and care for it. Mother would start out by explaining the planting process for each of the crops she had determined to plant that day such as potatoes, cassava, peas, sweet potatoes, tomatoes, etc. These were not merely makeshift or experimental gardens, but they provided for our very existence and livelihood. They kept us alive, clothed, and sheltered, and even at our young age, we were very sentient of this vital endeavor. She would demonstrate the way the hole had to be dug out, the spacing between the holes, and lastly the planting. As soon as she was through with this, she would pair us up and we would immediately begin to plant as she had shown. We went from garden to garden, planting and weeding, until the day was almost over. On other days we would prune the banana plantations and the cassava trees.

Some days were exciting as we watched the development of our own gardens. Other days, however, were challenging. For instance, one day, as I was pruning the cassava plants, I heard loud hissing and vibrating threats passing through the dry, tall grass at the very edge of our garden. My first thoughts were the usual garden rats digging up our sweet potatoes. With my hoe in hand, I marched over to the potato garden to vent my anger on those rats! Seeing that there were no rats in the potatoes, I returned to the cassava plants. As I resumed the pruning, my mother's voice echoed through my mind from the instructions she had given us that morning. I hadn't paid much attention until she warned us of the hissing sound from what she thought was a Puff Adder, a thick, heavily built snake with a large, flattened, triangular head, moving along the edge of the garden. This distinct and sudden realization sent a powerful jolt through me and I bolted in the direction of my mother's garden.

As I look back, our challenge was not so much in fleeing away from the invincible and vicious king Cobras and the African Puff Adders, but rather in having to deal with the invisible fear of an unnoticed attack. I do not know for sure what went on in mother's mind following the encounter, but she would gather us together and convince us that the snake had long since escaped and was scared of us. Her consolation, as I remember, fell on deaf ears because we knew how vicious these snakes were.

Another time that I vividly remember occurred one evening at about six o'clock. Mother had asked me to go to the village shop to buy some kerosene for our lantern, as we did not have access to electricity in those days. As I approached the little shop, I noticed a good friend of mine named Mukasa, along with a few children and the shopkeeper, were standing by the shop discussing what seemed to be an important matter. What had happened? Had a village elder died? It was not until I got closer to them that I learned that a big and long Cobra had been seen by my friend disappearing into a hole beside this very village shop. A few inquisitive elders, including the shopkeeper, were gathering information from my friend about what he remembered about this gigantic snake. Once they were convinced my friend was serious, they decided to find a quick solution to the problem which now had befallen the shopkeeper and the village.

"We should, first of all, pour kerosene inside the hole," suggested one village elder who was considered to be experienced and well versed in dealing with snakes. "Cobras can't stand the smell—it suffocates them."

One man, who I up to now consider to be the most courageous man I've ever met, volunteered to pour the kerosene in the hole. We all dispersed, but not so far as to limit my adolescent curiosity, and eagerly waited. He slowly poured in the kerosene and we watched, and probably inched forward a little more, but the snake did not respond. What had gone wrong? Could this be one of those mysterious snakes Grandpa had talked about one evening as we gathered around the fireplace? As these thoughts ran through my mind, another elder who had not uttered a word came up with another idea.

"We should pour hot water down the hole. I've done it before and it really works," he said, enthusiastically.

Although this was a new idea that none of the village elders had heard of, they decided to try it as a last resort. The same courageous man volunteered to pour the boiling water into the hole. As soon as the water hit the bottom of the hole, a vicious angry snake about 20 feet long shot up from the hole ready to vent its anger towards anyone and anything within striking range. I had seen and participated in killing a ton of snakes before, but never had I witnessed such a tall, angry black Cobra! I remember seeing it standing on its tail for about twenty seconds, and later fall to the ground. This snake had put on a magnificent spectacle for the evening, as good as any of those American adventure shows I was fond of. And to this day, those who were there still tell this story to their families.

Chapter 8

IN SPITE OF the civil war, hunger, crime, and horror around my family, I think God had some way of allowing me to enjoy some normalcy and pleasure of youth. To contrast those memories of darkness and hysteria that we experienced, my brothers and sisters and I were given rich childhood adventures to reflect upon in our adult years. We were not completely stripped of innocence and exuberance. Recalling the great snake adventure, for instance, still brings a smile and slight yearning for my youth. It was a wonderful way to grow up.

African kids have always made their own toys, and we were no exception. Most of my friends in our neighborhood, had had an experience designing their own steerable wire vehicle from recycled materials, and some of these were amazing. My favorite toy was the one my best friend, Mukasa, made for me after I promised to share my bread with him. It was a little truck that I steered from a wheel mounted on a tall pole which was attached to the front wheels.

My buddy started the designing phase with two different thicknesses of bendable steel wire, bending and forming the scraps into body shapes and panels using strips of black rubber cut from discarded bicycle inner tubes. The rubber strips kept the structure tightly bound while allowing for maximum resilience. The second phase was designing the steering wheel that also served as a push stick. The steering itself was easy but the pole had to be tall enough to accommodate our height, but not so heavy as to tip the vehicle sideways. The wheels were made from tires rescued from trash heaps cut into circles. This was a cool way to make a truck with little material. It was intriguing because at least we were making our own design decisions, something kids from the modern world could hardly lay claim to. In fact, all the boys I played and hung out with showed marvelous ingenuity in improvising toys, tools, and soccer ball surrogates. Trips to the trash dumps sometimes were as exciting as a trip to the mall is today. Hours could be spent there seeking some great find which could be used to build some great item of boyish entertainment. My soccer ball was made out of bark peeled from the banana trees. I'm still impressed by this ingenuity. It was always necessary to be creative with our toys when none were available, and this is how we made do.

Chapter 9

"GOD HELPS THOSE who help themselves" is an old adage that mother repeated very often during the harvesting season. With much pride and joy, we would each bring home the food we had individually planted. As we roasted the corn and the peanuts around the charcoal stove, we reminisced about the numerous challenges and the fear we had encountered in raising our crops. Mother would gather us around and have each one of us give a quick update on our garden assignments. Having done that, she would decide which of our crops needed quick harvesting. If any of my siblings needed help, we would leave our gardens behind and devote a few hours, or even days, to accomplish the task at hand.

In addition to gardening, we raised a few ducks and chickens, an activity that I enjoyed immensely. Mother again would assign all the poultry chores like she did with the family farm. In the evening my siblings and I would all go to the nearby well to fetch water that we would use for cooking and for bathing. I loved to go to the well, and so did my siblings and friends. The well provided the social setting in which we mingled with our friends and played all sorts of cultural games, including soccer.

Just as we enjoyed these adventures we also let our adolescent impishness run away at times. Many of us got into trouble, particularly when our parents discovered why it had taken us that long to report home on time. Mother, smart as she is, would first ask us to honestly tell her why we were late. Fearing to tell her that we had been socializing, we would come up with all sorts of excuses such as, "the line was too long," or "a strange man cut through the line and threatened to beat us up if we questioned his motives of pushing our containers out of the way." Although the excuses seemed believable, mother would insist she wasn't convinced and would give us another chance at explaining what we had been doing all that time. If we didn't tell her the truth immediately, she said, we would all spend the night outside. None of us wanted to go through that scary experience. We did not want to expose to mother our incipient laziness.

As soon as darkness closed in, the stray dogs looking for an evening meal would besiege our kitchen. We would all panic, cry, and then beg mother to open the door and tell her the whole truth. As soon as mother re-opened the door, she would lead us to our small living room and chastise us for being dishonest. Following a lengthy chastisement, she would spank us with her notorious bamboo cane and send us to the little study room, lit by candlelight, where she checked our homework. According to my recollection, this was the most difficult part of the evening because we didn't want to upset mother, who was still raging with anger. This is the moment when we all wished we had done well in our class work to avoid further punishment.

Mother was a great teacher, the greatest teacher I've had. She would introduce a new subject or lesson with distinct passion, and I thought it was fun to watch her work her way into it. Mother's enthusiasm would radiate through her voice inflection, and her face would beam with excitement. She was the consummate actor when she took the stage. My task was to listen very carefully, and be prepared at a moment's notice to explain to her the concept she had just taught. I remember paying attention most of the time, although there were occasions when my attention would divert to other things. This would make mother angry and frustrated. She would ask me to come forward, and then would proceed to spank me with a bamboo stick. From then on, I learned the importance of paying attention to my teachers while in class. Mother was taught by strict Catholic nuns, who believed in the old adage, "spare the rod and spoil the child," as the only conceivable way to educate a child.

Chapter 10

ASIDE FROM THE daily domestic chores in which we were expected to excel, mother also made sure we succeeded in school. This was not hard to understand as I grew older because I was cognizant of the fact that our family circumstances did not provide many options. She wanted us to excel in school and, poor as she was, she was determined to invest her meager salary in our education.

Our school sat on an acre of land, surrounded by mango trees. Occasionally Mrs. Babukiza would take my class out and have us sit underneath the tree that was adjacent to our classroom and tell us a story. It was during one of these unforgettable gatherings that she recounted a tale that has since then stayed with me. In this tale, ten villagers who had never been to a big city made plans to go there together. They were each distracted along the way, and in the end, only one of them made it to town. This story engaged my energies more completely than any other childhood fantasy. Even though we lived close to Kampala, mother rarely took us there and as a child, I obsessed about Kampala, the capital city, with its glamorous cars, trucks, and buses. My little mind could not understand how only one man out of the ten made it to town.

Police Children School comprised of three sections: A, B, C, and each section consisted of grades one through seven. A classroom was designed to hold up to forty students, but might hold as many as fifty students due to the transient nature of the community in which we lived. The buildings were fairly robust with heavy glass windows, sharp stone-plastered exterior walls, and asbestos roof tiles which leaked whenever it rained. The floors were cemented, but could have used some renovation due to the potholes which were filled with dirt. Each time a classmate of mine stepped through the holes, dust would fill the air, triggering a chorus of sneezing and coughing.

Each morning at 5:30 a.m., we would wake up and go to the farm, then return home at 7:30 a.m. to get ready for school. Our classes commenced at 8 o'clock. At exactly 7:45 a.m., a warning bell would ring and, in my family, that meant finding our pens, pencils and books. It also meant hurrying to school to avoid arriving late.

No one wanted to be tardy. Arriving late to school was taboo because latecomers were severely punished by the headmaster. Some students, realizing that they would not make it to school on time, would skip school. Although this choice seemed logical, it just exacerbated their problems because the school demanded that they present a letter explaining why they were absent. Knowing their parents would be upset, some students would turn themselves in to the ruthless headmaster. Many stories had been told of how he would jump on his old scooter and launch a surprise attack on pupils that would hide in the fields to skip school. The pupils would run for dear life when they heard the noise of the approaching scooter. Those who were caught were severely punished. These were, of course, exciting stories if you were not one of the culprits.

One day, I arrived late and had to report to the headmaster's office. My first eye contact with him was enough to give me a mental picture of the imminent catastrophe. I couldn't hide my fear and began crying, wishing I had surrendered my breakfast when the bell rang. He pulled out his cane and the ordeal begun. Because I was such a little fellow, he held my hands and started the whipping. It was so painful and, even though the whipping lasted a couple of minutes, it was enough to swell my buttocks for an entire week. As I remember, it was at that time I decided I would never arrive late again.

A lot is expected from a teacher's son, and as I reflect upon my experiences, this was indeed a tough challenge. School lasted four months, but those four months were mentally and physically exhausting. I remember worrying about my grades the day my teacher handed me my report card. I also wanted to get a good grade in my English class, a subject that interested mother the most. Mother would always remind me that, if I learned English well, many doors would open up for me and that one day I would be able to go to a good college. Mother's reasoning didn't make sense to me. This was a very hard language for me to learn, and the words were difficult to pronounce. I would have not counted it among my favorite subjects. Besides school, no one ever spoke it in my community and neither did mother at home. Young and ignorant as I was, it was extremely hard to understand what my mother knew or to even consider the future. It was difficult to grasp mother's vision which appeared to be so distant and way beyond reach.

What I dreaded the most about my English class was my strict teacher who never permitted us to speak Luganda or Swahili, the local languages spoken in the community. In fact, she would have our class monitor write down the names of those who had spoken the local vernacular during her absence. Knowing that I was a class clown and a chatterbox, I would insulate myself from the expected trouble by reviewing my class notes. This goal, however, was usually short-lived because somehow I would mumble a word or two in the local vernacular, and get myself in trouble.

Upon her return, the teacher would ask the monitor to turn in the culprits and then ask them to step up to the front of the class as she read out their names. Once we were all gathered around her table, she would pull out her cow horns she kept for this purpose, and adorn our little necks with them. Interestingly enough, these heavy, stinky, and ugly cow horns, with a string tied from one side to the other, hung in such a manner that our classmates called us names and started mooing. We looked like the legendary Shaka warriors getting ready for a traditional warfare. And to add to our embarrassment, the odor was so pervasive that all we could do was hang our heads and hold our breath. In fact, the stench was so overpowering upon my return home from school that none of my siblings had to ask how the English class had gone that day because they knew I had been under those stinky horns. It was later in my life that I eventually grasped why mother had emphasized that I learn a language that had no bearing to the local languages we spoke in the community.

Chapter 11

THE UGANDAN EDUCATION System to this present day is patterned after the British school system. This system was introduced by the British when they declared Uganda a British protectorate. In 1937, the Uganda Technical College started developing into an institution of higher education, offering post-school certificate courses. In 1949, it became a University College in a special relationship with the College of London. It soon became a College for the whole of Eastern Africa, offering courses leading to general degrees of the University of London. Education was eagerly sought by rural farmers as well as urban elites, and after independence, many villages, especially in the south, built schools, hired teachers, and received government assistance to operate their own village schools.

In my day, Ugandan students commenced school at the age of six and attended seven years of primary school education. At the end of the seventh year, all the pupils in the country took a comprehensive primary leaving examination. The successful students would then proceed to a four year lower secondary school. At the end of the fourth year, they would take the national ordinary level examinations. Those who passed the "O" level exams would proceed to two final years of upper secondary school or Advanced level, and later to college upon satisfactorily passing the pre-college classes. Those who failed would be doomed to retake the entire year. At the end of that year, they would take the test again and hope they passed this time.

I remember how stressful it was for me, and for the other thirteen-year-old students to prepare for a national examination. We all knew that after seven years of school, we would write the Primary Leaving Examinations, or the P.L.E. as we called it. We all knew that this was a day of reckoning. Mother called it the "day of harvest." It didn't really matter how well one had excelled in school in the previous years. The smartest kids studied just as hard as everybody else in class in order to qualify for the few secondary school slots available in the country.

None of us wanted to disappoint our parents. Mother had left no stone unturned in her quest of educating me. If I failed, she would be disappointed. If I passed, she would be proud of me. I remember overwhelming panic and my heart pounding as each passing minute brought me closer and closer to my first examination. My heart was pounding so hard I could feel it in my feet. At about 8:30 a.m. the supervisor would beckon us in to take our seats. Our desks were immaculate, as we had all spent the day before washing them and scrubbing off any visible written words. The Ministry of Education wanted to give a fair chance to all the candidates and mitigated this risk by having the invigilators check our hands and pockets for any suspicious notes. On occasion, some dishonest students would be caught cheating and would be disqualified. This meant retaking the examinations again the following year. At 8 a.m. we would all walk into the testing center, and sit in our designated places. We sat about two meters away from one another and were each given a registration number. The supervisor would come in about 10 minutes early to match each pupil or candidate to his or her own registration number.

At about 8:35 a.m., the Supervisor and two assistants would pull out the examinations from the envelopes. To assure us that the envelopes were intact, they would be held up high before the students and, using a pair of new scissors, the envelope would be cut open. Then, with all eyes fixed on him, the Supervisor would hand the examinations to the two invigilators, who in turn, majestically distributed them to all the students. At exactly 9 a.m., the little bell would be sounded, marking the commencement of the exam.

The first five minutes were the hardest for me. I was unsure about the first three questions. However, as I proceeded, I began to recognize the questions, and that seemed to boost my poise and confidence. We were tested in English grammar and comprehension, Math, Science, and General paper; which included Geography, Civics and History. The exams lasted two days. I had done my part, and now it was up to the graders to decide the outcome of my performance.

Three months later, as I was walking around the neighborhood, I ran into a former classmate who told me the Primary Leaving Examination results had been released, and they would be displayed at my old primary school. My heart started racing like it had never done before. It was now a matter of hours and I would know how I had performed. By the time I arrived home, mother had already heard the news about the release of the results, and upon seeing me, teased me about what the outcome would be. I did not want to think about how I had performed, but I could not avoid the topic. My little brothers and sister kept bringing up the topic over and over again. I do not remember sleeping that night because I was anxiously awaiting the news.

The following morning I walked up to the school. As I look back, it was the longest walk I had ever walked, not because of the distance, but rather the fear mixed with anxiety that was rolling around in me. I knocked anxiously on the headmaster's office door. As soon as he opened the door, he unfolded the good news. "You passed!" he said, "We just have to wait and see what school will accept you."

I ran home and, with a sigh of relief, I announced the good news to mother. She was so excited! I had not seen her that excited in the longest time. She hugged me and later prepared the best meal I've ever had.

Some of my friends were not as fortunate, and I sympathized with them. In life, you win some and lose some. This time I had won big, but I was still very far away from my long cherished academic dreams.

Chapter 12

WAS RAISED IN the Catholic faith and religion played an important role in our family. Mother says as soon as I was born, the parish priest, upon learning of my birth, came up to the hospital and christened me Vincent. Mother does not recall ever suggesting this name to the priest, but the priest might have surmised it suited me well.

Christianity was introduced in Africa by the Colonialists, and my maternal grandfather embraced it when he was a teenager in the 1920s. In fact, he was later hired by a Dutch Catholic priest as a porter to take care of his yard and also the convent adjacent to the parish. As time went on, my grandpa got more and more involved in the church activities in the community, and gradually won himself the trust and confidence of the parish priest.

Grandpa says that, one day, he heard a sermon given by the parish priest in which he invited the congregation to seriously consider sending their children to the local Catholic seminaries to be trained as priests. This sermon had such a profound impact on grandpa who quickly decided to send one of my uncles to the local seminary. In the early 60's, Fr. Benedict Muduku, my uncle, graduated from seminary and was set apart as a full Catholic priest. I therefore grew up in a staunch Catholic family.

Prayers were a must in our home, and even lasted longer when Grandpa came to visit. During one of his visits, after a drink or two, he would start chanting in a strange language what appeared to be old church hymns. It was only later that I discovered he was singing in Latin. I'd indeed considered him to be the cleverest man around, until one day, I inquired out of curiosity what the song in Latin was about. By custom, children are not supposed to ask elders questions. I could tell Grandfather, in deep consternation, had to really ponder his reply. "My grandson," he said, "I do not know. I wish I did. I memorized these hymns when I was young because Mass was recited in Latin." It did not make sense to me that Grandpa had spent all that time memorizing a hymn he never understood. Not even the congregation understood the archaic Latin hymns. I cannot even begin to imagine how frustrating it must have been to attend church and be expected to understand mass in Latin. But like many other devout Catholics in his community, he participated in these services because he had a deep-seated faith in God.

Every Sunday we would all wake up early and get ready for church. The church we attended was about three miles away and we ran into a third of the congregation on our way there. I visited and played with my friends while mother chatted with the other mothers shepherding their flocks to services. I enjoyed going to church every Sunday; except for one unforgettable experience.

Mother had woken up early as usual and had prepared us for church. She had given our favorite morning treat of a banana to my little sister and me. We soon embarked on our journey to church. The parish was surrounded by a grove of Mahogany trees and, on occasion, some village passers-by would stop to watch the legendary baboon that jumped from tree to tree with a rope tied to his waist.

Stories had it that the Dutch Catholic priest had rescued this baboon from an irritated mob of villagers. Apparently the village elders, concerned that their crops were under serious invasion, had decided to set some traps to catch the pack, but to no avail.

Then one day, a family in the village discovered a baboon had been caught in their trap. Before they could kill it, the priest came to its rescue and since then had kept it as a pet in the surrounding trees.

On this particular day we passed under the trees by the chapel. Unbeknownst to us, the big, hungry baboon was eagerly awaiting for a good Samaritan to feed it. All of a sudden, it swung out of the trees, carried me up through the air, took my banana out of my hands, then it threw me on the dirt road. I sustained a few deep scratches from the attack. Because this incident had happened in a split second, it caught mother off guard. Terrified and overwhelmed as she was, mother kept falling in the very same spot in her attempt to get away from this vicious attack. My little sister did not move but screamed at the top of her voice, forcing the priest and part of the congregation to run to our rescue. The priest took me to the local clinic that was run by the nuns who resided in a convent across the street from the parish. I was too young to comprehend how close I'd gotten to dying, but I am indebted to those that rescued us. Although I was terrified by this experience mother would often tease me about it and often we would both laugh until the tears came. Other than a few scratches the only thing hurt was my pride.

We did not have many church activities except for the classes we were supposed to attend which were offered by the Catechist. Sometimes a friend of mine and I would go to the church in the evenings to be trained as alter boys. This was a prestigious assignment to hold because you got to know the parish priest, and also wear the beautiful church robes.

As I grew older, I spent my school holidays at the parish with my uncle who was a Catholic priest and served as an altar boy during mass. I even considered enrolling in a nearby seminary, but this idea gradually faded out of my mind. It would be many years later that I finally understood why I struggled making that decision.

Chapter 13

A LTHOUGH I HAD passed my primary leaving examinations, I was not enthused to attend a boarding secondary school. I attribute most of this resentment to the sad anecdotal information I heard told by my peers who had gone through the experience before me. Each of their tough experiences had weighed so heavily on my mind that, at one point, I considered the option to defer my place for the upcoming year. Stories they told about bullies, disgusting food, homesickness, tough class assignments, competition, and many more, made me think it was safer to stay home and face the Parish baboon. I felt committing to this school was tantamount to signing away my social independence and freedom to a bunch of bullies and teasers. I had talked to mother regarding my concerns, hoping she would change her mind and consider sending me to a day school. She listened and patiently waited for me to complete meandering about my worries. When I was done, she looked at me, and the expression on her face was enough to send back the message she had on her mind. Her desire was for me to follow through with the plan.

I knew she was right. She had worked hard and sacrificed in order for me to have this opportunity, an opportunity which didn't come to many. As I look back on my thoughts I realize how my thoughts centered on me rather than the hopes, plans and prayers offered by a loving mother for her son. She knew the better the education her children had, the greater the possibility was that they would no longer have to worry as much about food, shelter, and safety. I had forgotten she had done all the worrying for us already.

I do not remember us having a further conversation about the decision, except for the night prior to my departure. She assured me many people had traveled down the same path I was about to embark on. They had gone through what had appeared to be an endless dark tunnel, and finally walked out stronger on the other side than when they had come in.

She gave me all the books I needed for school, a little pocket money, and extinguished the lantern lamp. It was indeed a long night! I had never made the choice to leave home by myself, and I had never lived responsibly on my own. But there was no other way. I had to leave. I now think my mother lying in her bed also had the same feelings, "He has to leave, there is no other choice."

I woke up early the following morning, to find mother preparing food for me. A few minutes later, my siblings woke up and they all reminded me I was leaving that day. Maybe it was because they wouldn't have to put up with me any more. As soon as breakfast was over, my mother and my siblings escorted me to the Kampala railway station. I had been to this train station before to see some people off, but on this day I would be the one to be seen off. The station master soon rang the bell. I began crying quietly, and so did mother. It was so hard to bid my family farewell. In a few minutes I would be heading out on my own on a twelve hour journey to live with students I didn't know. I would not be able to speak my local languages. I would try to speak my broken English and some Swahili, and hope that I would be understood.

Stopping at every station made the journey very long. On the train, one met all sorts of people; good and bad, poor and rich, sane and insane. Mother had warned me to be careful with my suitcase and so I placed my legs on top of it to avoid any surprises. The people around me spoke different languages, many of which I recognized. There were so many passengers that if for some reason you abandoned your seat to use the restroom, you immediately lost it. A few fights broke out, but the police officers on board quelled them. I was now exposed to the challenges that come with leaving the comfort zone.

My courage had already been put to test once before when mother sent me on an urgent errand to take some medicine to my ailing grandfather in the village named Maseke. That morning, I was supposed to catch the only bus to return home. On many other occasions prior to this, grandfather had accompanied me to the local trading center, but this time he couldn't do it due to the effects of old age. Grandfather had an inner clock and conjectured it was 5 a.m., the ideal time to prepare me for the one-hour journey on foot to Nkokonjeru, the local trading center where I was to catch the bus. He led me to the door with his lantern lamp, providing me with enough light to see the dirt road. Then he gave me a big hug, and wished me well. The moon was covered with rain clouds, so much so, that I could hardly see my hands. The dirt road was full of rocks and ditches which threw me off balance with each step I took. I kept my focus on the road, hoping there wouldn't be any snakes crossing my path. On my right and left I was surrounded by trees and bushes. In the distance I could hear the whining and howling of wild stray dogs. This caused my hair to stand on end, and I quickly picked up my pace. It was now survival for the fittest. I suddenly remembered the stories mother had told of being chased by a pack of wild dogs while we sat by the log fires roasting corn. This was that same rugged road, and I wondered how mother had been able to run on it while being chased. My heart begun to pound sporadically and soon it started to rain and it poured down on me with a vengeance. Luckily, I made it to the trading center, just in time to catch the bus. I couldn't wait to share my experience with mother.

That had been three years ago, and that experience was in the past. Just as I had done then, I had to believe in myself. If I didn't, no one would. Only the brave survived here.

After twelve hours of no sleep, I finally arrived at the new secondary school.

Chapter 14

THEY SAY THAT "experience is the best teacher," so my "best teacher" taught me to endure and to adapt to the new circumstances.

I arrived at Masaba Senior Secondary school at about 12 o'clock on a school truck that I boarded at the Budadiri local trading center. I was exhausted. I was not the only new student arriving that day. There were many new students like myself arriving at school. As soon as we arrived, the older students ran over to the truck and started shouting obscenities to us. This was just the beginning of the hazing and teasing. Initially, I was intimidated by these obnoxious boys and wished I could get out of my predicament. One way to do it, I thought, was to buy some time by letting the bigger boys jump off the truck first, but I quickly realized that this plan would not work. This teasing and bullying was a ritual that was embedded in the culture of this school. Each new student had to equitably share in this rite of passage. They had to break us in.

Nervous as I was, I gathered some energy and jumped off the truck. A group of older students ran over to where I was standing and started shouting at me, calling me all sorts of names. They were so vociferous and out of control that I thought that those moments would be my last. They then demanded that I give them the goodies I'd brought with me.

These boys were big and mean, and emaciated as I was at the time, I could not think of even one possible way I could have defended myself against the smallest of the group. By now, I was willing to give them whatever they demanded just to save my life. No one, not even the teachers, came to our rescue. It was only later I found out that each new student went through this tough experience. "You have to be tamed," they said, although I thought they needed it much more than we did.

When the first wave of hazing and intimidation was finally over, I was assigned to a hall, Manafa hall, which was named after Manafa river, one of the biggest rivers in Bubulo County. Upon my arrival there, the second phase of the teasing began. The upperclassmen who resided in this hall opened my suitcase and ate the remainder of my homemade treats. As I was contemplating my fate, a strange-looking, big upperclassman, who introduced himself to me as my cubicle mate, approached me. He officially pronounced I had passed the first test, and there were many more ahead of me. Frightened as I was, I asked him in my broken English if he knew what I could do to avoid such harsh treatment. His response was, "share with me your pocket money and you'll live like a king". I did just that and my life was spared for the next four months.

Although school was difficult, my gravest challenge was acclimatizing myself to this new regimented lifestyle. I woke up at six o'clock and went to the dining room where I learned the food was rationed to all the students based on some caste or seniority practice. The upper-level classmen took the lion's share, and everybody else got the remaining fragments. The share one was allocated by the table leader was commensurate with ones class rank. All freshmen had to be on time in order to be guaranteed any food. Our breakfast meal was one cup of sugarless porridge, which we were well accustomed to due to the sugar shortage in the country. At 8 o'clock, school began. At 11 o'clock we had a recess and another at 1 p.m. Our lunch was comprised of bean stew and posho. The posho, or *ugali* in Swahili, is prepared by boiling water and vigorously stirring the maize flour into a thick, smooth mush. At about 4 o'clock, school ended and we all headed to our dormitories to grab our forks and spoons and head back to the dining hall where the same menu was served for dinner. Following dinner, for those interested in sports, there was soccer, basketball, badminton, and field hockey. As much as I dreaded the upperclassmen, I realized I couldn't do without them. There was no way I could survive in my new environment without acquiescing to them.

For the first time, I was introduced to Chemistry, Physics, Social Sciences, Agriculture, Commerce and Biology. Chemistry and Physics were particularly difficult to learn because we do not have scientific terminology in our native languages. You had to completely adapt to a new way of thinking; and that necessitated tweaking one's cognition. I had never been exposed to this scientific outlook toward life in my culture. I had lived a very simplistic, subsistent, and unscientific lifestyle, and quite frankly it was extremely difficult to merge any aspect of my cultural upbringing to these new scientific concepts. The four brutal months finally came to an end and I knew in one more day I would return home to see mother and my siblings. Sleeping was hard that night as I recall because of the anxiety. I looked forward to the long and arduous eight-hour journey back home. At 8 o'clock the following morning I boarded the truck, and the driver dropped me off at the trading center. I walked straight to the railway station, boarded the train and headed for home. I was now very experienced and ready to immerse myself in the rich, cultural tapestry that makes Uganda so vibrant. I could not wait to take a peek at the Owen falls hydroelectric dam, right by the source of the river Nile. In spite of its beauty, the dam had once served as a repository of Amin's victims. Divers had been called at one point to remove thirty bodies which had blocked the intake duct, thereby hampering the supply of electricity across the country.

Mother was waiting for me the day I arrived at Kampala railway station and I could tell how anxious she was to see me. I had caught sight of her for a little while before she saw me. When she finally did, she ran towards me, and gave me a big long hug. It was a wonderful, familiar, comforting embrace, richer that I had anticipated on the long ride home. Wiping a few tears from her eyes, we started walking home. Her first question to me was whether I had asked for permission from my headmaster to go visit my father's tombstone. Father had been buried 5 miles away from school, and mother always insisted I go pull the weeds around his grave site, a very poignant event for me and for her, even at that tender age. After that solemn moment, mother quickly caught me up on how everybody was doing, both at home and within our community.

Upon our arrival at home, my brothers and sister greeted me with big hugs. I tried as best I could to maintain my "older brother face," but inside I had welcomed their embraces as well. Mother invited us to the table where she had some delicious food prepared for us due to the occasion. The whole lunch conversation revolved around my experiences at school and my classes. We laughed a lot as I narrated my funny experiences, and they empathized with me when I recounted my sad ones. Indeed there was a lot to talk about; a lot had transpired. I remember that we were all happy to see each other once again; and the old saying, "charity begins at home" really hit home. This sublime feeling was deeply rooted into my heart as I began to understand its significance. The old village stood still. Nothing much had changed. Now that I'd returned home, I was looking forward to visiting with my old friends to find out how they had survived their first term at their respective secondary schools.

Chapter 15

SOMETIMES IN LIFE one develops a sentimental attachment to things and places. And so it is for me. I was very happy to be back home in my community where I was loved, where I felt the most comfortable. My brothers were eager to tell me what had transpired in the home and in the community during my four-month absence. My mother, on the other hand, had bought me a new hoe and was ready to send me to work immediately on the family farm.

I remember that my brothers told me some funny anecdotes, and we laughed a lot. However, some were sad, because some of the elders in the village had passed away. Most of the deceased elders had played a fundamental role in my upbringing and I wished I'd attended their funerals. That evening I visited their widows, as was the custom, and relayed my condolences. We were taught at a very young age to look up to the elders with respect. Literally, they were like your parents and grandparents. These were men and women who by virtue of their mere existence were respected for the hardships they had endured and overcome in life. Some had fought in the Second World War against Hitler, in the seventh regiment of the King's African Rifles into which many had been drafted. In fact, most of them, like my late Uncle Sefani, still held on to the uniforms with great honor and dignity. But most importantly, they were the cultural pillars of our community. They resolved disputes, mentored young men, and instilled discipline. With utmost respect we saluted them whenever we crossed paths on our way to school or church. They were always inquisitive about the progress we were making in school, or in sports. They knew our parents, and knew our names.

As the days passed, I ran into my old classmates from our local school who had just returned from their boarding schools. We reminisced a lot about our tough experiences with the bullies at our respective schools and also our classes. Each of us trying to make it more terrible than the others, we wondered how we had survived. Would we be able to stand up to all these challenges? We did not have any answers as I remember, but we were proud to be in Secondary School.

I spent the remainder of my vacation working along side mother in her garden. I was so grateful for each minute I spent with her. Mother was particularly impressed with the energy with which I worked. She was inquisitive about my experiences at school, and imbued me with confidence to carry on, reiterating that in spite of the difficulties I had undergone, things would get better. She shared with me her tough experiences when she was a student, the bullies who would shave part of her hair at night while she slept, and how embarrassed she was when she discovered it when she woke up.

"Bullies have been around since time immemorial," she would say. "Don't let them rob you of your college experience. Just have faith in God, Vincent. He will be at your side." I felt encouraged by her words, but wondered if I had the same amount of faith in God to implement her resolute advice as I stood alone against those vicious upper classmen.

After a very exhausting day of work, we would come home, prepare a late meal, and, after eating, we would take naps. In the evening, we would go play and mingle with our friends. My favorite pastime was soccer. We would begin playing soccer at about five o'clock until 6:30 p.m. when the sun went down.

Chapter 16

T HERE SEEMED TO be an immediate sense of bonding and support system which developed within the group of my friends. We had all gone through tough times together. Others had lost family members, homes and other precious things during those years. My friends and I decided to be supportive of one another amidst our trials. We were still vulnerable to the endless teasing and bullying at our respective schools, but as long as we were still alive we were determined to complete our first year. Like all good things, summer came to an end rather quickly that year. With profound sadness, I stopped by all my friends' homes to bid them farewell. It was painful to deal with this moment, and I tried as much as I could to hold back my tears. Mother took me to an open market where she purchased for me a couple of white shirts, two khaki shorts, and a pair of shoes. It was difficult for me to sleep that night. I was scared.

School began and I stood up to every challenge. I was now well versed with all the survival tricks and so my body was acclimatized to the school environment. What helped me to survive during the hard times, were the few letters that mother would write. I was encouraged, strengthened and more determined to succeed after reading her words of counsel and love. Around mid-term of each year, parents were given an opportunity to come visit their children. Unfortunately for me, mother never made it because she couldn't afford it. It was hard to see the other students running to greet their visiting parents. But we boys had a special association. We stuck together. My friends, without a selfish thought, invited me to share the companionship of their parents' visits. Those parents too knew the circumstances, and were kind and loving to me as any parent would be.

The toughest moment that year, had to do with a new program that was reinstated by the World Food Program across most of the secondary schools in sub-Saharan Africa. Because of the severe drought which had struck most countries of Africa with such unprecedented magnitude at the time, the World Food program had stepped in and donated a substantial amount of agricultural equipment in an effort to help schools become self sufficient. Our school was not an exception, and consequently we were the recipients of hoes, shovels, and axes.

At a school assembly, which was attended by a World Food Program (WFP) coordinator for the area, we were assigned a plot of land which we were required to till and later plant crops. As I remember, the solution was quite logical. This program was vital to the schools to augment their meager food supply. I particularly was enthused about the entire plan because of the gardening skills I'd acquired through mother on our farm. I looked forward to pitching some of mother's farming wisdom to this endeavor. That day I was assigned a team, and the activity began.

No sooner had I started digging than I discovered that the new hoes were blunt. Each time my hoe hit the ground, it would bounce high, a testament to the unprecedented drought which was relentless in its intensity, beating down on the eastern province at the time. I saw malnourished children with bloated bellies devour what should have been life-saving cereal and then die because their weakened systems could no longer digest it. The common cold and seasonal flu became deadly diseases in nutrient-deficient bodies.

We exerted all the energy we young skinny boys could muster in order to take care of our assigned plots. We planted beans and cassava. By the time we were done, my hands were filled with innumerable blisters. Although I had been accustomed to blisters working on our family farm, these were extremely painful. We had no gloves, shade, or even shoes as we worked under the sun sometimes causing the temperature to feel closer to 106 degrees Fahrenheit.

Life afterwards became miserable and almost unbearable. Taking showers or bathing was painful, and so was writing and playing handball and basketball. For the first time I realized how useful my hands were to me. Surprisingly, after a month of digging, my hands got used to it. I didn't suffer from the blisters and such for the remainder of the term.

Chapter 17

I T IS DIFFICULT for me to this day to comprehend how I survived my first year at Masaba Secondary School. I arrived home a week before Christmas and everybody was happy to see me again. My mother, brothers, and sisters were all in good spirits and we were all happy to be reunited again. I'd passed my first year and that thought, in itself, was indeed comforting. Christmas was just a few days away, and I was anxiously awaiting the big party.

Everybody in my community looked forward to celebrating Christmas. It was such an encompassing celebration. It did not matter whether one was a Muslim or an Atheist, a Catholic or Protestant. We were all united and looked forward to the festivities. Christmas was also a day of peace and reconciliation, as neighbors put personal grudges behind them to celebrate Christ's birth. On Christmas day, everybody generously shared food with one another. Mother would put some of our food in a dish and have us run it over to the neighbors, who in turn reciprocated by sending us back with whatever they had prepared for the occasion. Although Money was scarce and we rarely received gifts, mother's attention, devotion and sacrifices throughout the year to send me to school, feed my brothers and sisters, and care for the home was gift enough from her. To this day the gifts I can now afford to give to mother will never satisfy my indebtedness to her for those many years of struggle. There were many parties and many activities going on in the community. This jovial mood would proceed on through New Year's Day.

Our family preferred attending the Midnight mass with all our neighbors. This marked the beginning of Christmas, and at midnight we all participated in singing Christmas carols. We returned home at about 3 o'clock in the morning. As my siblings and I retired to bed, mother would begin cooking our Christmas meal. The meal included roasted pork, chicken, beef, matooke, rice, chapatti, and sweet potatoes. The aroma caused my mouth to water in anticipation of the lunch and dinner meals I anxiously awaited.

The one and a half month holiday ended. I had enjoyed my experiences here and would soon go back to school to endure the grueling challenges.

The long four years of intense schooling culminated into a comprehensive national exam. Our examinations dragged on for one full month. We were tested in all subjects and each exam was mentally exhausting. The hardest ones for me were the chemistry and the physics practicals. Part of the Chemistry test, for instance, included setting up the apparatus and following all the requisite steps. This was tough, and many students, including myself spent half of the time panicking. The idea behind the chemistry tests was to determine whether the students were able to determine if a solution before them was either acidic or alkaline. I hated the smell of gasses, and the titration experiments. But now what I liked and disliked about the science subjects did not matter. Passing was the only goal I had in mind.

After a month of what seemed like ceaseless torture, the examination period finally ended and we packed our worldly possessions and left the school for good. I do not particularly remember lamenting my departure, for I was ready to get out of there as fast as I could. But I will never forget the profound lessons I learned from these tough experiences. I was definitely more knowledgeable than when I came in. I'd entered this second phase of my education as a half baked country boy, but now I was leaving as an educated and refined teenager.

Three months later, I was at home listening to the evening news when I heard the results of all the testing were completed. It was not until the next day when I found out I had passed with no distinctions, but with good grades. Mother gave me a big hug and with a few tears running down her cheek, she commended me for enduring the four years of stress and challenges. Even though mother had attributed all the success to me, I knew deep down that it was Heavenly Father who had blessed me.

Chapter 18

A LTHOUGH MANY OF these childhood events were those common to most young boys living in central Africa, there was one dark, ominous, ever present specter lurking over all people, young and old in my country of Uganda. It was an unusual contrast of boyhood adventures, family experiences, schoolyard exploits and the total fear of living under a regime based on blood and terror.

I had heard the stories of torture, corruption, graft, robbery, forced labor. And I had experienced it up close with the murder of my father. Just a short distance from where I had lived was the infamous Makindye barracks where events occurred which cannot be described in this book. Mothers, fathers and others would be taken there never to be seen again.

Living in constant fear of dying, being taken away to who-knows-where, and fearing the same for your family and friends did take a toll. The older a person grew, the greater a threat he or she was in the paranoia clouded minds of Idi Amin and his minions. A late knock at the door wasn't just a knock. A car driving slowly by was something that made your heart beat faster. Sounds in the distance at night made me wonder who might be missing come the next morning. Although this did create adult concerns for me as a young boy, I cannot imagine the thoughts, fears, and concerns my mother carried in her heart and mind. The strength to carry on for her family had to be God-given.

From the day my father was killed to the day Idi Amin was overthrown through a concerted military effort of the Ugandan National Liberation Army and the Tanzanian Military Force in 1978, the International Commission of Jurists estimated that more than 400,000 Ugandans had been killed and many more were unaccounted for.

Idi Amin was Africa's Saddam Hussein of the 70s. As soon as he reinstated himself, he expelled all the Asian-born Ugandans out of the country, and in the ensuing years, declared himself life President. His eight-year rule was characterized by economic decline, social disintegration, and massive human right violations.

As I grew older, it became apparent to me that many innocent people were disappearing on a daily basis. No one, not even the victims' families, dared to openly discuss the circumstances that led to the disappearances. At night, mother would whisper to us the rumors she had heard concerning the arrests. She appeared very nervous, and her countenance was just enough to instill more fear in us. I'd witnessed personally a few incidents before where the State Research Bureau would come to the door, and with no search warrant, enter into a house, and start beating up the victim so severely before his family. They would then put the half-dead victim in the trunk of the car, and that would be the last time that family would see their loved one again. We were so suspicious of one another because Idi Amin had a very efficient spy network within the country. The perpetual undercover maneuvers by Idi Amin's henchmen sowed fear, distrust and apathy, sending shockwaves through the country. Many civilians had been secretly hired by the State Research Bureau to help identify citizens who opposed the government. Ugandans were even scared of their next door neighbor.

My first vivid memory of the State Research Bureau personnel was when a teacher at my school tried to discipline the son of a State Research associate. The student fought back vehemently and sent for his father. Within minutes, the State Research Bureau personnel in their notorious vehicle arrived at the school, arrested the teacher on the spot, put her in the trunk of the car, and drove her away to an unidentified location. She showed up several weeks later with a deformed face. She was so lucky to be alive.

Another experience that is still vivid in my mind occurred in 1976. We were dismissed from school early that day because Idi Amin had been invited as the guest of honor at a Uganda Police graduation ceremony at Nsambya. I was so excited to take a peek at the man that everybody in Africa was so afraid of, the man who declared himself "life president," and who had other strange titles like "the Conqueror of the British Empire." In fact I had seen people wearing shirts bearing those very words, with a picture showing several Britons carrying a chair on which sat Idi Amin, held up in the air. I don't know to this day how these British men ended up with such an odd assignment. Amin, or to use his nickname, "big daddy," weighed over 300 pounds, and I cannot comprehend how they got him off the ground and for how long he was carried.

I was also looking forward to seeing the leader of the Police Band, Inspector Okello, a very flamboyant man whose entire body bounced with rhythm as he led the band. He had a majestic march, and his feet never seemed to touch the ground. My favorite part of his performance was when he would throw the baton very high and, after a few steps, catch it again with ease. This man had exceptional coordination. The ceremony began on schedule and the young police privates started marching for the "passing out" parade. Everything seemed to be going well. The Police band was playing some of my favorite tunes, and I was indeed having a good time. All of a sudden, I heard some gun shots and a few seconds later, a huge explosion knocked me off the ground into the confused crowd. "What's happening?" I mumbled. I tried to flee the incident but each time I tried to make any effort, I was pushed down and run over by the crowd. The crowd was visibly disoriented and running in every direction. Idi Amin's escort vehicles were shooting towards the crowd with what appeared to be machine guns without regard for men women or children, just to shoot and kill. I remember seeing blood everywhere. I had jumped over dead and wounded people, crying in deep agony, lying all over the stadium, in my own attempt to escape the chaos alive.

I somehow made it through the crowd, jumped over the fence by the entrance to the stadium, and ran as fast as I could to our home. Mother had gone out looking for me and, as soon as I arrived at home, my siblings gave me mother's emergency orders in unison. "Mother said that as soon as you come home, we should all hide underneath her bed." I was the first to huddle underneath mother's bed and the rest of my brothers and sisters followed suit. Mother had tried to find me, but had failed, and had decided to come back home. As she walked into the house, she locked it and inquired if I had come home. We all in unison responded that I had returned, to which my mother replied "Blessed be God!" I can hardly fathom what my mother was going through. There she was again, looking for one of her precious family members who was missing amidst a backdrop of such terrible, lawlessness, and deadly circumstances. I wonder what she was thinking as she returned home after not finding me. It was so similar to that familiar search for my father just a few years prior, a search that for her turned out so tragically. I know why her words were, "Blessed be God!" because it was God's hand that preserved me that day for something I did not understand then. She joined us on the floor as we silently listened on the radio what had just happened. An anti-Amin faction had tried to assassinate the president, but had narrowly missed, and instead shot down his top bodyguard. In retaliation, Idi Amin's bodyguards had ruthlessly acted in kind, shooting at the crowd, which they thought had masterminded the plot. This incident was indicative of the anti-Amin sentiment that was building up in the country towards the presidency. The opposing faction had sent a clear message. Unfortunately this attack had failed, and like history has shown, it is surprising how lucky tyrants like Amin narrowly escape assassination plots hatched to release a people from violence by using violent means.

Kyaligonza, who participated in this failed assassination plot, had this to say about the incident: [5]

"Later we made the most daring attack on Amin at Nsambya Police ground, where we tossed grenades towards him as he was passing by the police officers. We missed the target but we were able to injure some of his escorts and driver. We withdrew through Kibuli, Mtajazi and onto Kabalagala, and finally went to Buziga past Makindye and finally to Najjanankumbi. The town was thrown into serious panic and a lot of people were arrested and tortured."

Another accomplice in that assassination attempt was a man named Kayiira who says, "On June 10, 1976 three grenades were hurled at the presidential jeep at Nsambya Police barracks. Idi Amin's driver was killed, prompting Amin to drive the jeep up to Mulago hospital. Panic-stricken soldiers opened fire into the crowd killing more than 50 people." [6]

As I recall, many people supposedly linked to this abortive assassination attempt were killed. It has been reported as a result of this failed attempt 2,000 Ugandans were killed in a bloody purge in the days following.

As for me and my family, we were spared, and we never talked about it nor probed around for more details relating to the incident, except for the prayer my mother offered the day after the incident had occurred. My family and I will forever be grateful to Heavenly Father for saving our lives.

---

5 Kyaligonza, Matayo. "Agony of Power." The Daily Monitor/Book Review 25 Feb. 2007.

6 Kibirige, David. The Daily Monitor 7 Mar. 2004.

The Acholi and the Langi tribes were particularly objects of Amin's political persecution because Obote and many of his supporters belonged to these tribes. Idi Amin surprised the entire world when he ordered the murder of Luwum, the Archbishop of the Church of Uganda, whom he had accused of conspiring to overthrow him.

It all started in 1976 when tension between the Church and the state reached a climax. Religious leaders, including Archbishop Luwum, met to discuss the deteriorating situation and asked for an interview with Idi Amin to share their concern about the escalating atrocities meted on the innocent citizens. The President denied the nefarious acts and reprimanded the Archbishop. In 1977, Idi Amin trapped the Archbishop by claiming that he had been conspiring to overthrow him.

On the 8th of February 1977, the Archbishop and nearly all the Uganda Bishops met and drafted a letter of protest to the President and asked to see him. A week later, on the 16th of February, the Archbishop and six bishops were publicly arraigned in a show trial where they were publicly accused of smuggling arms into the country to overthrow the government. Archbishop Luwum was not allowed to reply, but shook his head in denial. The President concluded by asking the crowd, "what shall we do with the traitors?"

The soldiers replied, "Kill him now."

The Archbishop was separated from his bishops. As he was taken away, Archbishop Luwum turned to his brother bishops and said, "Do not be afraid. I see God's hands in this."

The next morning it was announced that Archbishop Luwum had been killed in a car crash. The truth was that he had been shot because he had stood up to President Amin and his government. He was killed just a few months before the centenary celebrations of the church of Uganda, an anniversary which marked the martyrdom of the Ugandan Anglicans nearly a century before. Many Christians, including my family, mourned the Archbishop's death. Who would be next? Many embassies severed their diplomatic relations with Uganda, and called their diplomats home. Some were reassigned to other countries around the world.

University students, fed up with these ceaseless atrocities, demonstrated and some were killed by the government's Special Force unit. Many university professors fled the country. All the ministries were run by Idi Amin's henchmen most of whom were corrupt, uneducated and incompetent.

I will never forget the 1977 Kampala Clock Tower firing squad dubbed "Death in the Afternoon." On September 9th, 1977, Amin publicly executed 12 people he accused of plotting against his government. Those executed at the Kampala Clock Tower included Y.Y. Okot, former Chief of Education; John Leji Olobo, Senior Relations Officer of Ministry of Works; Elias Okidi-Menya, former General Manager of Lake Victoria Bottling Co; Garison S. Onono, former Principal of Bobi Foundation School; Julius Peter Adupa, former teacher in Lira; Ben Ongom, businessman; Abdalla Anyuru, former chairman of the Uganda Public Service Commission; Leutnant Ben Ogwang, former intelligence officer at Malire regiment; Daniel Nsereko, former assistant commissioner of Police; Peter Atua, former principal officer with Luzira prison; E. N. Mutabazi former superintendent of prisons; John Kabandize, former Senior Superintendent of Prisons.

Firing squads were the order of the day, and served as a lesson to any opposition groups to give up the struggle or be subject to instant death. Executions were supposed to be attended by all civilians and no government or civilian offices were open to the general public on those days. Those were only the public displays of tyranny. There were hundreds if not thousands of "unofficial executions" carried out in these times by the government. And everybody knew it. And unfortunately so did the leaders of what is called the free world. Whether they could or should have done something is for the future to decide.

Countless numbers of prominent Ugandans perished in the dungeons in these makeshift prisons. In a memorandum to African leaders after fleeing into exile, the former education minister, Edward Rugumayo, said: "Too many nations regard what is happening in Uganda as an internal matter. Is systematic genocide an internal matter or a matter for all mankind?"[7] Like all Ugandans, my family with no place to go, accepted our fate, and heavily counted on Heavenly Father's mercy to sustain us through these calamitous times.

In order to aggrandize his military plans, Amin decided to trade Uganda's cash crops for the state-of-the-art military equipment including jet fighter planes. Cooperative Unions who worked very closely with the farmers in their respective provinces promised "top shilling" for their coffee beans. Many were pessimistic and wondered if the government would ever make good on that promise. Most of the farmers waited for six months before they would be paid by the cooperative unions interspersed in the country. And they could do nothing about it. It was so expensive to make ends meet due to this scarcity. For instance, sugar in my family was reserved only for special occasions. Most of the sugar, soap, and cooking oil industries were owned by the former businessmen who had come from East India in the late 1800s. Once expelled from the country in 1972, these once thriving factories that once upon a time had provided the indispensable essential commodities were now silent and unproductive.

The Indians had come to Uganda early from British India to do work in "Imperial Service." They were clerks, bankers, factory managers and played a significant role in the economy of the country. There was always a rift between what was called the "Asians" and Ugandans. An air of Indophobia existed long before Amin came to power. In the late 1960's President Milton Obote proposed an increased participation by native Ugandans in the once restricted arena of Ugandan business. Restrictions began as early as 1969 as a result of the Committee on Africanization in Commerce and Industry.

7 Martin, David. *The Ledger* 3 Sept. 1976: 31.

When Idi Amin came to power he exploited this division for his own purposes. Similar to how Hitler used the Jews for advancing his evil purposes, the Indians soon became scapegoats for all that was wrong with Uganda. They were attacked and called *dukawallas*, the Swahili word for "shopkeepers," and were required to adhere to restrictive work permits and trade licenses.

This separation became final on August 4, 1972 when President Amin ordered Uganda's 80,000 Asians to leave the country within a strict maximum of 90 days. He said he had a dream in which God had told him to expel them. He later distributed their businesses to his cronies, a form of unjust enrichment.

So almost overnight the Indians were gone and left a void in the business, manufacturing, and economic sectors of Uganda. Whether the Asian influence was restrictive and closed to native Ugandans is another issue. The fact remained my country suffered because of this rash, severe, and irrational decision by a man with unrestricted power and less than national interest as his goal.

Every essential commodity was rationed. For instance, four times a year, the government would supply local shops with "government sugar" to be sold to the general public at a subsidized government price, and we anxiously jockeyed for position within our neighborhood stores to partake of this rare opportunity. The queues spanned several blocks from the shops and there was a lot of commotion as some dishonest people always invented ways of jumping ahead in the line. In order to increase our chances of at least procuring a kilo of sugar, mother would have us all go to different shops. A few shopkeepers hoarded the sugar and soap. They would sell half of their allocation to about twenty people in line and falsely declare that all the sugar had been sold. They would in turn sell the hoarded sugar on black market, usually asking ten times more than the original price. Uganda, at this point in time, held the record for inflation in Africa. Prices for goods and services across the board rose from 20% to 50%. Prior to this, Uganda had never known famine, for her agricultural wealth, exports of coffee, cotton, copper, and her infant industries had allowed her, for the most part, to be less and less independent of the outside world. As if that was not enough, Uganda's foreign reserves were at their lowest; the government coffers were drying up.

Although we dreaded the self serving and selfish hoarding practice, it was not an easy one to fix. Merchants had to make ends meet, and were determined at all costs to carry on this nefarious act at the expense of the masses, even if it meant death if caught by the government. Who were we to judge too harshly? What would we have done?

Chapter 19

ERHAPS WHAT MADE Idi Amin stand out as a notorious dictator was what has come to be known as the Entebbe Rescue Mission, which was by far the most successful rescue mission ever carried out in this century. I remember, clearly, the late night and early morning of July 3 and 4, 1976, because mother woke us up to what appeared to be the end of the world. From our home, thirty miles away from Entebbe airport, we could hear massive explosions.

Originally codenamed *Operation Thunderbolt* by the Israeli Defense Forces, the operation was retroactively renamed *Operation Yonatan* in memory of the Sayeret Matkal commander Lieutenant Colonel Yonatan "Yoni" Netanyahu, who was killed in action. Three hostages were killed and five Israeli commandos were wounded.

The Entebbe rescue had begun on June 27, 1976, when four Palestinian terrorists forced Air France flight 139 with 246 passengers to land in Uganda. Their purpose was to demand the release of 53 convicted terrorists held in Israeli prisons. The hijackers released the French crew and non-Jewish passengers, and kept 105 Jewish and Israeli hostages. The hostages had been moved from the aircraft to the old terminal building of the airport. A 48-hour deadline was set to meet the terrorists' demands or executions would begin. Idi Amin was involved in this hijacking plan and hosted the hijackers.

The Israeli government, known for its unwavering stand of not negotiating with kidnappers and terrorists, announced that it would enter into negotiations with the hijackers. This was a clever lie designed by the Israelis to buy them time to consolidate a seemingly impossible military strategy. The hijackers bought into the Israeli trickery and issued a new ultimatum for 1 p.m. on Sunday, July 4th.

The Israeli airplane capable of this operation was the C-130 Hercules. On July 1, an Israeli General, Dan Shomron, presented his plan to the IDF Commander and also Israel's Defense Minister. It was an extremely high-risk operation. Israel fully expected strong resistance, including that which could come from the Ugandan Army itself. While General Shomron circled above in a Boeing 707, the first of the five C-130's dropped down and landed at 23:01. Led by Lt. Col. Yonatan Netanyahu, the cargo carried two jeeps and the now famous black Mercedes, a perfect copy of dictator Idi Amin's personal car.

President Amin, never missing an opportunity on the world stage, had previously come to the airport and met with the hostages. Despite his smiling assurances and promises, the hostages knew this man did not represent their welfare in the least.

Two additional Hercules carried reinforcements and troops assigned to carry out special missions, such as destroying the Migs parked nearby. A fourth Hercules was sent to evacuate the hostages. The air package included two Boeing 707s, one to act as a forward command post and the second to be outfitted as an airborne hospital.

Despite the fact that the runway lights were on as they started their descent, the Israelis managed to land undetected at 11:01 p.m., only a minute short of their planned time. The Israeli soldiers fooled the Ugandan soldiers at the airport. In fact, they saluted the Israeli driver in the Mercedes mistaking him for Idi Amin. Meanwhile, another Israeli group stormed into the airport and ordered the Israeli hostages to take cover. The Palestinian hijackers, who did not understand the commands, remained standing and were shot to death. The assault on the terminal was completed three minutes after the first plane landed. Once all five C-130's were on the ground, the rest of the 200-man assault force secured the roads to the airport, destroyed the parked Mig jet fighters to prevent pursuit and even refueled one of their aircraft using Entebbe's fuel supply. The hostages were removed to the rescue plane within seven minutes of the assault. Tragically, the force commander, Yoni Netanyahu, was killed by a sniper as he led the hostages toward the aircraft. IDF forces suffered no other losses in the rescue. The last plane took off at 00:40.

Sadly, one hostage was not rescued. Dora Bloch, a seventy-four-year-old woman with dual British and Israeli citizenship was murdered by Ugandan army officers. She had been taken to Mulago hospital when food got stuck in her throat while she was kept hostage at Entebbe airport. Bloch's son, also a hostage, was not allowed to come with his mom. According to Tom Gawaya-Teggule, a Ugandan journalist, Dr. James Makumbi checked on his patient, Dora Block in Mulago hospital. She had been assigned to ward 6B. She told him she was feeling better than she had ever been since coming to Uganda. Satisfied with her condition, Dr. Makumbi continued on to ward 6C to check on his other patients. On his way back from 6C, he first heard screams then watched helplessly as Dora Block was dragged away by two men dressed in civilian clothes, and carrying pistols. The two men were later identified as Major Farouk Minawa, head of the SRB, and Captain Nasur Ondoga, Idi Amin's chief of protocol. Dora Block screamed continuously as she was dragged and carried downstairs, leaving behind her cane, handbag, shoes, and dress. Patients, staff and visitors crowded at the doors of the wards to see what was happening. They all knew she was going to her execution. They couldn't do anything, for interference meant death. She was thrown into a black Peugeot 504, still screaming as it sped away.

Her body was dumped in a swamp near Namanve, and a free-lance photographer, Jimmy Parma, who took snapshots of it, was killed by the SRB. In 1979, after Amin was overthrown, Dora Block's family returned to Uganda and exhumed her body. The best proof of her identity in addition to the pathologist's report, were her nylon socks which had remained intact through the years.

The other Israeli defense squads accomplished their missions successfully. This mission struck a blow at international terrorism. The world was reminded that freedom is a value which must be fought for in every generation.

A classmate of mine who lived in Entebbe told me that residents there were terrified on the night of July 4 when the Israeli commandos struck Entebbe Airport. One of the residents in a flat on Nakiwogo road, Mrs. Norah Mawanda, was awakened by the sound of machine gunfire, at about midnight. She woke up her husband, Lawrence Mawanda. When they looked through the window, they could see the airport was in darkness. From their vantage point, they could see bullets flying allover the place.

Lawrence thought it was a coup, but Norah was led to believe it was the Israelis. Within 90 minutes the Israelis had left, after planting bombs at the airport which continued to explode through the early morning. Amin's ego had been severely crushed, and somebody, somewhere had to pay. The notorious State Research Bureau was out to investigate who had been involved.

As it turned out, Lawrence Mawanda was a deputy officer in charge of Navigational Services at Entebbe Airport. He had confirmed through a BBC news bulletin the veracity of the events surrounding Israel's raid of Entebbe airport. Lawrence had not been at the office on the day following the raid, and his phone calls to his colleague, Muhindo, were not returned. He decided he would immediately go check on him, after serving breakfast to their two children, Michael, aged 2, and Tony, aged 9 months. As he served breakfast, Lawrence told Norah he would not be long. Norah excused herself and hurried downstairs to do some domestic work. That morning, the SRB agents had started a round up of all the airport navigational staff, and the first person to be arrested was Lawrence's boss, Fabian Rwengyembe, who had just returned from a honeymoon. The second person on that list, unfortunately, was Lawrence. The SRB agents walked to his door. He was still feeding his children. They grabbed him, and led him away. He did not resist or utter any sound. Too young to know what was happening, Michael apparently felt excited at being left alone, and started messing up the table. Surprised at the noise emanating from the children who were supposed to be eating breakfast, Norah decided to go upstairs to check on them. The table was messy, filled with spilled over food, but Lawrence was not there, although his spectacles were still on the table.

"Some men came through the door, and took father away," said Michael. When Norah dashed outside, she was just in time to see the agents' car going through the gate. By the time the agents reached the nearby Katabi barracks, Lawrence was dead. Nails had been hammered into his head, and the rest of the body had been battered beyond recognition. His colleagues were killed later.

These wanton killings aroused an indescribable tension between Amin's totalitarian government and the bewildered civilians. The international community was not immune to Amin's massive massacres. They wanted to probe into Amin's reign of blood and terror.

In July of 1971, two Americans, Nicholas Stroh and Robert Siedle, began to investigate reports of the massacres among provincial tribes during the coup that brought Idi Amin to power. Stroh was the son of a wealthy Detroit brewer. He had once worked for the Washington Star, the Philadelphia Evening Bulletin, and other U.S. newspapers. He left his job to work as a freelance journalist in Africa. On July 9 1971, he and Siedle, a sociology lecturer at Makerere University, went to ask questions about the massacre at Mbarara barracks. They saw the second-in-command, Major Juma Aiga, a taxi driver at the time of the coup and now a District Commissioner in Toro. Stroh and Juma got into a heated argument. The two Americans were hacked to death. Their bodies were later doused with gasoline and burned. Nicholas was 33, a former Peace Corps volunteer in Africa. The two men were buried in a shallow grave nearby. Major Juma was later seen driving Stroh's blue Volkswagen in Mbarara. When the American Embassy began inquiries a week later, the bodies were dug up from their grave, put into sacks and burned in the barracks. Their remains were then dumped in a river. The car was burned and thrown into a mountain valley.

In April 1972, in unwilling response to American efforts to find out what had happened to the two men, Amin appointed a judicial inquiry headed by a British judge, Mr. Justice David Jeffreys Jones. After reading a report of the killing written by one of the men involved who had fled, the judge managed to trace the car. Amin was furious and ordered the inquiry to be halted. Justice David Jeffreys who had witnessed what had happened to the Chief Justice, completed his report, resigned and left the country. He had concluded that Ali and Juma were responsible for the two deaths. Amin dismissed the judge's findings, calling them the result of a prejudiced mind.

The State research Bureau that Ali Towelli headed was set up as a military intelligence agency. It was a state within the state, run by men who did not possess the hearts and feelings of human beings. A lot of them had never been to school. They were illiterate and could hardly speak a word of English. But these were the men in charge of the provincial planning committees and security committees and controlled all the other local administrative business units. Their leader, Farouk Minawa, a Major in the Army and a vicious man, was Amin's top confidant. He was from Amin's tribe. The Bureau members were not on the official payroll. They did not have to be. Amin paid them handsomely as a reward for gathering information and pinpointing those who had to be obliterated. In addition, they looted and plundered from the rich civilians. They were given handsome sums to spend when they went on overseas missions. Many of them were between the ages of 22 and 35. They had two to three cars each in overseas missions and several in Kampala. They lived a first-class life that no other civilian could afford. They did not wear uniforms but were decked in flamboyantly red or green shirts with flowers, bell bottomed trousers and dark glasses. These repressive secret agents operated everywhere in the country. They did not have to operate covertly as they had once done in early 1971.They had gone public and all the civilians knew of their illicit mission. They were no nonsense people. They arrested people in offices, on the streets, as well as at public functions, and in restaurants. They drove Peugeots, Range Rovers and Datsuns with UVS as the number-plate, followed by the organization they belonged to which was designated numerically. Amin never gave open orders while in their presence. But he had made up certain phrases that were only known to them. For instance when he said, "Give him the VIP treatment," he meant death after torture. Another euphemism he used was "Take him to *Malire* and *Kalasi*" which means "death" in Nubian.

In October 1978, the East African countries were willing to fight and oust a common enemy. The Tanzanian force, with the backing of Ugandan exiles, waged a war of liberation against Amin's troops. Tanzania had been sympathetic to the upheavals in Uganda, and had in fact hosted former Ugandan exiles, including Yoweri Kaguta Museveni, the current president of Uganda, and Milton Obote. As the battle intensified, Amin requested military help from his ally, the Libyan President Muammar al-Gaddafi, and soon Libyan soldiers were sent immediately to help him. Despite the help from Libya, on April 11, 1979, Kampala was captured, and Amin fled with his remaining forces through the Eastern and Northern part of the country.

On that day, it was announced the Uganda National Liberation front had evicted Idi Amin out of the country.

We were so happy and we all hugged each other. It was a universal jubilation. Unfortunately, many of our friends had not survived the war, and that in itself was sad. We all looked up to the Tanzanian soldiers who had sacrificed their lives so that we would be able to enjoy the long awaited freedom. We invited them to our homes and gave them all we had. A brotherhood between these brave soldiers and the Ugandans developed. These Tanzanian soldiers symbolized freedom, hope, trust and love. I remember that many girls in and around Kampala fell in love with them and married them.

A few days later all the prisoners detained in Uganda's death camps were released. The international community was shocked to learn how Idi Amin and his henchmen had put to death the innocent victims. The so-called prisoners went through indescribable torture and excruciating pain before they were killed. Their road to death and final peace was not an easy one. As soon as they were arrested, the victims would be brought straight to a prison where their ordeal would begin. In a democratic country, a convicted person at least goes before the courts to prove his side of the story. Unfortunately, these innocent victims never saw a day of justice. Many did not even know why they had been arrested. I paid a visit to Makindye prison, being the closest to where I lived. I find it difficult up to this day to describe it to anyone. Even in this record of my experiences, it does not seem proper to describe what I saw and heard there. Idi Amin was an evil, vicious man who somehow was able to create an atmosphere of the utmost evil that is usually buried very deep in a man's heart. But my heart goes to all those innocent civilians who were maliciously killed.

Immediately after Amin's removal, the Uganda National Liberation Front (UNLF) formed an interior government with Yusuf Lule as president. All of Uganda was thankful that the reign of Amin had finally ended. Many Ugandans were willing to put the gruesome past behind them and steer forward to a peaceful future. This new government adopted a ministerial system of administration and created a quasi-parliamentary organization known as the National Consultative Council (NCC).

Unfortunately, the new government ministers held different political ideologies. President Lule was replaced by President Godfrey Binaisa who was in turn removed in December of 1980 over continuing dispute about the powers of the interior presidency. Thereafter, until the December 1980 elections, Uganda was ruled by a military commission. The December elections returned the UPC to power under the leadership of president Obote.

Chapter 20

I WAS ACCEPTED TO Kampala High School in 1984 to study social sciences. I was proud of my scholastic achievement and enjoyed all my classes. I met new friends with whom I studied and discussed the events of the day. In the meantime, my sister Annet had been accepted to Nsambya Hospital nursing school only a few miles away from home. My brother Martin had decided to attend a Catholic Seminary and looked forward to becoming a Catholic priest. The rest of my siblings, Patrick, Francis, and Stella were finishing up their Primary school education.

Although everybody seemed to be doing well, my mother's health had deteriorated considerably. She had injured her back while working on the farm and I wondered how long it would take her to recuperate. Considering the long hours mother had put in on the farm, it was foreseeable that she would, in the long run, sustain a back injury. It seemed she used all her vitality and strength to care for and provide for her family, and now that the immediate difficulties had passed, it was hard for her to give more.

In the meantime, the new government under President Obote was rapidly losing its popularity. Rumors had it that President Obote had bribed the Uganda Electorate commission to declare him winner in the elections. Under the Obote government, the security forces killed a lot of innocent civilians in their efforts to stamp out an insurgency led by Yoweri Museveni's National Resistance Army.

Violence around the country particularly in the southern parts of Uganda had picked up momentum and it appeared as though the clock had been rewound to the Idi Amin days. Although the government didn't publicize the guerilla warfare with the Obote regime, those who had relatives in the invaded areas would share what they had heard concerning the ongoing civil war.

Once again the struggles of my country became a personal experience for me. It was about four o'clock in the morning. From a distance I could hear army men kicking people's doors and angrily repeating *Funguwa Mulango,* a Swahili command meaning "open the door." I later learned that this was a government-led operation to catch men who were participating in the guerilla warfare against the government. Once the door was opened, the inebriated army men with their guns cocked would demand angrily all men from ages fourteen take their shirts off and head out of the house. Many wives and their children cried amidst this terror, scared for their husbands and sons. As soon as they stepped out of the house, they would order the suspects at gunpoint in Swahili , *"Panda Gali,"* translated into English as "board the Swedish-made Scania trucks." Not knowing where they were going, or how much longer they would live, most of these men would board these trucks and would begin sobbing. These raids were randomly carried out within the outskirts of Kampala, and it was hard to tell which city would be targeted on any given day.

Upon arrival at the police stadium, the men would be ordered to sit down and await further instructions. I can imagine the terror and fear of these men and boys as the very stadium they were in had been the scene just recently of mass executions and other horrors. Over three thousand men per night would be brought there. At about 8 a.m., the army men would bring over thirty half-dead men, whom they claimed had been captured during the ongoing civil war, to identify from the three thousand men those they thought were part of the guerilla movement. They would order the men to line up and begin marching single file past the prisoners of war. Standing by these prisoners were some ruthless army men who would coerce the prisoners to point out those that they knew from the guerilla war. Some of these prisoners would be flogged to instill fear in them. The fiercest moment was when the men began marching past the prisoners. They were very nervous and very pensive. If a prisoner pointed you out, you were separated from the rest and taken away. Being taken away meant immediate death. Again these "witnesses" had to point out somebody. Failure to do so met additional torture and death to them and their families. The people they pointed out were most likely innocent of any crime. It once again begs the question, "What would I do?"

At about four o'clock, all the men that had survived the screening would be released. They would walk through the narrow gates and run for their lives. They ran as fast as they could because they feared the government troops would call them back. The run was symbolic of the freedom they had just won. It was like resurrecting from the dead.

By this time, it was obvious to most Ugandans that we were heading towards a civil war. Obote's men, who had been to the front line and had had several encounters with the guerillas, talked about how sophisticated they were. At the same time, Uganda's economy was in dire straits. The Ministry of Defense, which had once paid its army on time, started delaying the salary payments. This gave rise to plundering and looting of civilian assets and even occasional killings if the civilians resisted.

One evening, at about 9 o'clock, we were preparing to go to bed. A state of emergency had been declared and a curfew was reinstated. Suddenly someone kicked our door and my little brother started crying. I started shivering, knowing that we were about to die. *"Funguwa Mulango,"* he demanded angrily. Those were the familiar words which friends and others said started their journey of terror. They came as close to death as one could and yet survived.

We all looked at each other, not knowing what was to happen next. I was 18 years old and therefore amongst the age group which was taken and never seen again. The men again repeated *"Funguwa Mulango."* We were planning on pretending no one was at home when one of the marauders shot through the ceiling of our home. Knowing there was no way out, I volunteered to open the door. The raider kicked me a few times and demanded I give him money. At this time we were in the house, in one of the rooms. Each time I raised my head he would tell me to look down and threatened to shoot me if I made any further eye contact. I knew he had little patience and would shoot me there and then just to intimidate the rest of my family. Right at that time, he inquired where my parents were. I called mother, who was, by this time, incoherent and unable to come to the room. Her face was a mask of terror. As soon as mother revealed herself, the man grabbed her by the shoulder and threatened he was going to kill her unless we gave him all the money we had. I remembered that I had seen about 5,000 Ugandan shillings in one of the drawers in our bedroom. The money was equal to about twenty dollars and represented thirty days of work and savings for my family. I went back to the bedroom and gave the money to him. He put it in his pocket and left immediately. Again our lives had been spared. We would possibly have been shot to death had we not given him what he wanted. This incident, one of the most terrifying my family and I went through, was thankfully one of the last such dark events we would have to suffer.

In late January 1986, the National Resistance Army, under the leadership of Yoweri Kaguta Museveni assumed control of the country. This new government put an end to the human rights abuses of earlier governments and established a human rights commission to investigate previous abuses. Museveni also instituted wide-ranging economic reforms after consultation with the International Monetary Fund and the World Bank.

Chapter 21

THE REMAINDER OF 1986 was such a tough year, and students all over the country were seriously affected by it. Because of the ongoing civil war, many schools had been forced to shut down. Most classrooms had been reduced to ashes during the intense fighting between the National Resistance Army and the Obote government.

Studying was extremely difficult and there were days we never made it to school. I was worried because in less than ten months, we would have to take the advanced level examinations. My friends and I met and studied together and in March of 1986 we took our examinations.

After our finals, I interviewed for a job at Hotel Diplomat, a popular hotel in Kampala. I'd hoped they would hire me as a waiter, but I didn't get it. At the end of the interview, I was given a job in the laundry department. I was so disappointed, but consoled by the fact that it was the first formal job I ever had. Work began every morning at 8 o'clock. My boss would give me about 20 pairs of bed sheets and some soap and wished me a good day. We had a laundry room where all the dirty laundry was piled. When I checked in each morning, I would meet with my manager who gave me the requisite laundry soap and the bed sheets. These were seldom soiled bed sheets, and that simplified my task. I immersed all the bed sheets in a large basin, and started scrubbing them manually. We did not have any washing guidelines in place at the hotel, but the lessons mother had instilled in me came in handy. I would dip the bed sheets in the basin, soap them, and scrub them. Lastly, I would rinse them three times before placing them on a clothesline to dry. By the time I was through with ten hours of consistent manual labor, my back would be very sore, making it hard to stand. Before I called it a day, I would iron the bed sheets, and then wait for the supervisor to approve the work I had done. My manager was a slave driver, a micro-manager extraordinaire who never gave me any slack. However, I was consoled by the fact that the job gave us the financial boost that we sorely needed.

One of the perks of working at Hotel Diplomate was the free lunch they provided, which was the food left on customers' plates. My brothers and sisters would ask me what I had eaten for lunch, and they vicariously savored every meal. They wished they could eat there.

One cold morning as I was about to go to work, I heard a knock at the door. It was too early in the morning for any usual visitor, and I wondered who was at our door that early. As I opened it, I realized that it was my grandfather. He had taken the early morning bus in order to make his 8 o'clock appointment at the hospital. He had been diagnosed with cancer, and because he was weak, he needed one of the grandsons to accompany him. He was about 75 years old. And although he traveled the 250 miles from his home in Mbale, he needed help at the bustling Mulago hospital, which was usually packed with hundreds of patients waiting attention.

Mother woke up and gave me some money to take my grandfather to the hospital "I do not have enough money for your transportation back, you will have to walk home," she emphasized.

I helped grandfather get on his feet when I noticed that he was physically impaired. Giving him as much support as he needed, we both walked slowly to the taxi park. We took the first taxi available and after a dusty and bumpy ride we arrived at the hospital. As usual, it was crowded. But with some help, we made it through the crowd. We were on time and as soon as we sat down, one of the nurses led us to a ward where my grandfather was assigned a bed. We visited for a little while and I left.

As I walked the ten miles home in blazing heat that day, my mind began wandering. I meditated about grandfather's situation, mother's health, our meager finances and my job, and my future. "Suppose I do not pass, then what?" I pondered. In my country it could take up to one hundred and fifty days between taking the exams and knowing the results. Not passing meant my future was hopeless. But passing, although not guaranteed, opened other possibilities such as attending Makerere University, the only university at the time, or a professional institution around the country. As I was about to cross the road I saw a big signpost across the street. As I approached it, I read it. "The Italian Embassy—one kilometer ahead." Right at that time, I felt some strong inner feelings prompting me to stop by and solicit a job. "Maybe they need someone to mow their lawn. Just give it a try," I thought. Guided by those feelings, I anxiously walked to the gate and rang the door bell. A tall ominous looking fellow opened the gate and inquired what I wanted. I told him I wanted to talk to the caretaker of the Embassy.

"What makes you think he will have time to talk to you?" he exclaimed. "I have been working here for over ten years, and he has never talked to me." Before responding, he again interjected, "By the way, what makes you believe he will talk to you? Are you crazy? Don't you get it?"

I begged this man again to give me a chance. Out of frustration, he let me in. The compound was so beautiful and so was everything in my vicinity. I approached the inner door and courageously knocked. A white man dressed in a military uniform quickly inquired what I wanted. I mumbled something like, "Can I speak to the caretaker?" He did not respond, but went back in one of the rooms. While he was gone, I regretted entering this barricaded compound. What was he looking for? Was he going to throw me in jail? I was nervous.

He soon returned with another white lady. The lady was kind to me and asked me what I wanted. I told her that I was looking for a job. She told me that all the jobs had been taken. As I was about to leave she inquired whether I'd completed high school. I told her I had and that I was waiting for my high school results. She sat me down and told me to wait. She came back with a booklet and what appeared to be an application form. She said that the Italian Government was offering some scholarships to students like me to go on a study abroad program. She thought I would be a good candidate and promised to contact my high school. She told me to fill out the application form and return it in two weeks.

I was so excited and I remember running all the 10 miles home with the news. From a shaky, timid, and, should I add, scruffy-looking boy looking or pleading for any type of manual employment to an international student! At the time I thought how lucky I was. But now, looking back, I understand it was not chance or luck but part of a plan an eternal being had for me. When I saw mother I attempted to explain what had just happened but I was breathing hard and couldn't talk. She gave me a few minutes to catch my breath but did not move. Finally I broke the good news to her hoping that she would be as excited as I was. To my surprise mother was pessimistic. She thought I was pulling a trick on her and didn't believe me. It was not until she saw the application form and my passport forms that she finally started believing that I was serious.

In two weeks I returned he application forms to the Italian lady. She told me to check with her within a month. I was very introspective as I walked back home that afternoon. I really wanted to go to Italy, but I also realized that there were many students who were just as qualified as I was. If fact Italy was just a place I read about in books and sometimes saw in the movies.

I didn't even speak the language! I began to understand what mother felt. What chance did a little dusty Ugandan boy have for such an opportunity as this? I wondered if the Italian lady was just being nice rather than serious. All I had to do was to pray and wait. Each night I would pray with my family. Mother, who at one point had expressed pessimism, would include me in on the list of her many petitions during our daily prayers.

Chapter 22

THE WEEK THE "A" level results were released was the very same week I found out that I'd been accepted to attend school in Italy. It was a crisp Monday morning when I left home and walked to the Kampala Post Office to make the phone call to the Italian Embassy. When I phoned, Mrs. Cantone, the Italian diplomat, whose voice I recognized, answered the phone. I proceeded to ask whether the selection committee in Italy had furnished her with the list of students who had been offered scholarships to study at the SCM institute in Italy. She paused for a couple of seconds, and asked for my name. I was restless. Then she got back on the phone, and broke the news to me.

"Congratulations!" she said. You've been accepted. I couldn't believe what I had just heard. Through some miracle that is not yet totally clear to me, I had been offered the SCM fellowship to study in Italy. I was tongue tied, and overwhelmed with emotion. I immediately ran to Christ the King Catholic Church in Kampala, knelt and thanked Heavenly Father for blessing me with this colossal opportunity. It seemed it was a dream and I was afraid it would end. Why, out of all the Ugandan children who were smarter and richer, was I selected? I could not control my tears. Mother, with relentless tears flowing down her cheek, was barely able to speak. She too recognized God's hand in blessing her son with such a great chance in life. My brothers and sisters ran and gave me big hugs, and all wished me the best. I immediately pulled up a world map that a friend had lent me and anxiously tried to find Italy. I remembered from my geography class that Italy was adjacent to France, and once I located France it would be easy to find Italy.

"I found it, I found it," I exclaimed. The entire family quickly ran over to see Italy for the first time. Mother, upon seeing Italy, now wanted me to find the Vatican, the headquarters of the Catholic Church, the Holy See. It took us a little while to find it but when we did, she turned over to me and said as she pointed at the map, "Now son, remember to visit these sacred grounds and while there, buy me a holy rosary and have the Pope bless it".

"Of course mother, I will," I cheerfully responded.

I'd studied European geography with little interest while in Secondary school, but now I wished I'd paid more attention to the boring teacher. In less than two weeks I would be leaving my homeland for a year. I'd heard about the severe cold winters, the deadly blizzards, the snowy roads and wondered if I would survive them. I was also worried about flying. I'd been to the airport once but had never reckoned that one day I would board an airplane.

Leaving my native Uganda was not by any means an easy thing. Although I had encountered many challenges and patiently overcame them, I realized I was not ready yet to surrender a community which had nurtured and prepared me to become a hardworking and responsible individual. I knew from the bottom of my heart the old saying "East or West, home is best" to be true now than at any other time in my life. It now dawned on me any knowledge, moral values, respect and any other traits I had acquired to this point had been for my own good, and would be instrumental in guiding my life if I remained true and loyal to them.

On the other hand, I couldn't fathom a life without mother, my brothers, sisters, and friends. It was then I understood it was my family, the love we had for each other, the sacrifices and struggles we endured together which had preserved me for this moment. And most especially the daily prayers of a devoted mother which had buoyed me, had been both a shield and comforter for this moment. They had indeed been ever the best of friends to me and had been there for me through thick and thin. Now they would remain behind and hope the very best for me. Even though the future ahead seemed bright and full of adventures, it also loomed ahead of me, full of the unknown, unfamiliar and especially loneliness. I knew that where I was going was more significant than where I had come from or where I had been. As it got closer to the time to leave, my excitement and fears grew. The little boy fighting baboons, snakes and worrying about lions on the way to grandfather's, and witnessing some of the most terrible times in the world, was going to magically be transported to a completely different continent.

My friends came from far and wide to behold the lucky boy who would shortly be leaving the African world on a journey to a place far away and somewhat mystical to the point of bordering on mythical. Mother had referred me to an older gentleman who had been to Europe in his early years to give me counsel and advice about the European lifestyle. He was referred to as the "English Gentleman," a nickname he had acquired upon his return from London in the 60's. He gave me a pep talk and shared many experiences, both positive and negative, about England. He talked about the ceaseless rain in spring, the heavy traffic and the hot and humid summers, the snowy streets, and the fast pace of life. I knew that I could handle the hot summers and the ceaseless rain, but I felt like the snow and the cold temperatures were insurmountable. I had never seen snow, except in my world geography textbook. I was used to the slow pace of life, but the hustle and bustle that seemed to characterize most European cities exacerbated my fears.

Mother took me to a second hand shop in the neighboring town and bought me a tie, a pair of trousers, a shirt and a jacket.

My little brother, Patrick, gave me a new pair of shoes, in fact, his only pair he had resiliently acquired through his Saturday job.

Upon our return, I rushed to one of the rooms and tried my "new" clothes on. All my little brothers and sisters were eagerly waiting to see how I measured up. When I presented myself to them, they all cheered me and complimented mother, acknowledging what she had done for me. I did not wear my tie because I didn't know how to tie the knot. My brothers and mother asked me to walk back and forth to see if I fit well in my new clothes.

As I look back, that day marked a turning point in my life. For a long time I had yearned for a presentable shirt, a decent pair of slacks, a well-polished pair of shoes, a tie, but due to lack of money, I could not afford any one of the above necessities. Now here I was, and even though all my clothes were second or third hand, I was indeed indebted to mother who had again sacrificed all her shillings to elevate my life to this new social stratum. She later came that evening to my room and gave me a big hug. She didn't talk much, but looking in her eyes, I could see the waters of joy.

The following morning I went to the passport bureau to check on my passport. I remember meeting many young and older men, trying to secure passports for various reasons. Some were businessmen who traveled across Africa, Asia, and Europe looking for merchandise and could only carry out these enterprises with a passport. Very few young men like me were seeking passports for educational purposes. I later found out through my conversations that day, a passport was probably by far the most important document the country gave out to its citizens. Without it, it would be impossible for anyone to enter any foreign country. Because it was such an important document to have, the government carefully scrutinized all the applicants. A prospective applicant always began this lengthy process in his or her own village by taking a letter of acceptance from a host school to the village chief. These chiefs were hard men to meet with, and as I remember it took me over five trips to see him.

After a lengthy interview, he signed my application and referred me to the county chief. As I approached his residence, I realized that there were many people waiting to see him. He majestically walked to his office. As soon as he closed the door, we all squeezed ourselves in the lines and patiently awaited our turn. After a few hours, I walked in and as I reached my hand out to greet him, he rejected my hand shake, but instead asked me to produce my application forms.

He reviewed my papers with a lot of scrutiny and after reading a letter of recommendation from my village Chief; he asked me several questions about my family, my education and my trip to Italy. He paused for about five minutes and I could tell he was seriously scrutinizing my candidacy. His decision would determine either my eligibility or disqualification as a viable candidate. Finally, nodding approvingly, he reached for a pen and signed my form. He gave me directions to the passport bureau and dismissed me.

Now I was just a few moments away from acquiring a passport. When my turn finally came, I handed all my papers to a stern-looking gentleman who looked at them and approved them. He told me to step aside and when he returned he handed me my first passport. I looked at it many times and tears ran down my cheeks. I opened it, read it, smelt it, kissed it and later put it in my bag. It was now crystal clear that I would be traveling to Italy in just a few days. I had stood in line for eight hours and my patience had finally paid off.

I came back to a surprise party mother had thrown in my behalf. We were all in a jovial mood. Lingala music was playing in the background and the smell of the delicious food filled our little house. Along with my family, community leaders and the village Elders came to see the boy who was going off to a far away land to go to school. About 300 in total came by our house to wish me well. In my village a success by one member was success for all and a real cause for celebration. The elders reminded me of my childhood days and how naughty and noisy I was before I was a teenager. Each of the elders, as is the custom, gave me some words of wisdom and encouragement. They were well aware of the challenges that lay ahead, but filled me with confidence. I took their words of wisdom and courage very seriously. It then occurred to me it was not safe to look into the future with eyes of fear, but rather with confidence and hope. From my European History class I remembered Winston Churchill had once said something to this effect, "the farther back you can look, the farther forward you are likely to see." My early experiences in life had molded and nurtured me, and I looked with optimism at the journey that lay ahead.

When all the visitors had left, mother spent about an hour with me going through my small baggage, making sure I had packed all my earthly possessions. I also spent a few hours with my brothers and sisters, reminiscing our childhood experiences and cracking jokes about the adventures that were about to unfold in the ensuing days.

Retiring to bed that evening was so difficult. I was worried about traveling alone on the airplane. I was insecure about my communication capabilities, and even though I spoke and wrote English well enough, I spoke it with such a thick accent that I feared no one in Europe would ever understand me. In spite of that, I was silently proud of my accomplishments. I was proud of mother and what she had done for me. I was proud of my brothers and sisters for their immense love and support, the village elders for their words of wisdom and their optimism about what the future had in store for me. Lastly, but of course not least in importance, I was proud of the entire community that had immeasurably contributed to my upbringing. Each of these elders had literally played a part in it. The more I reflected upon their sacrifice which had been so instrumental in shaping and guiding my life, the more I was indebted to them. Indeed with their collective and unselfish efforts subtracted, I wouldn't be where I was now.

Mother woke me up at about 5 o'clock in the morning to get me ready for the long journey. I was advised to check in at Entebbe Airport at least two hours prior to departure time. Rose, my cousin, had recently married a successful gentleman who owned a car and who had insisted on driving me and my family to the airport.

After a quick and cold morning bath, I dressed up in my new attire, and boy, was I spiffy! It was almost unreal to imagine I would soon be embarking on the longest journey of my life. Mother had prepared a big breakfast for me, which included tea with milk, roasted peanuts, roasted sweet potatoes, and bread.

At 6 o'clock, Mr. Okol arrived to take us to the airport. We squeezed ourselves in his tiny car and off we departed. Entebbe airport, our destination, was twenty-five miles away from home. As I recall, the journey was bumpy and dusty, but most of all, very entertaining as we listened to mother's humorous stories. On the sides of the road, one could see the vestiges of the civil war. Dilapidated armored tanks and bombed army jeeps still lay in exactly the same spot which then had been the combat zone, shortly before Kampala fell to Museveni's liberation troops. These tanks had severely been demolished, and needless to say, there were no survivors. "Mother, did the neighboring villages survive this catastrophe?" my little inquisitive sister asked.

"No," replied mother, who knew a family in the area that had been massacred when that village was besieged and was undergoing constant bombings. These vestiges were so revealing and so touching, and the silence that ensued for a minute or so summed up how we all felt about our country's political problems. On the one hand, they quietly portrayed the plight of the innocent souls who had been killed, or forced to die in a politically motivated war in which they had no say. On the other hand, the aftermath of the war symbolized a new hope and quite frankly, the advent of a democratic government with humane leaders.

Within minutes we arrived at the airport. Panicking and shaking, I retrieved my small bag from the trunk of the car. My heart was pounding like it had never pounded before. I had been to the airport once with my class to watch the planes, but I had never dreamed of flying anywhere.

There were a few people at the airport, both black and white, all conservatively dressed. They commanded a lot of respect, and appeared to be experts or masters in their professions. Right next to them was me, the inexperienced country boy trying to fit in with this elite class. Across from where we stood, was the big Ethiopian Airlines Boeing 767 with a few engineers servicing it. Mother led me to a line where a lady weighed in my bag, checked my pockets and shoes, and invited me to join the rest of the passengers. When I looked back, mother was crying quietly, and even though I had earlier on promised myself that I would not join in, I could not hold back my tears. Leaving behind my mother and family was something I could not prepare for, or imagine the feelings of, until it happened. We did not talk much, but we quietly understood what each tear meant. Survival for the fittest, a saying that my English teacher had reiterated on many occasions in class dominated my mind. I wondered if I would be equal to the challenges that lay ahead. Whether or not I was physically, spiritually, or mentally prepared for the adventure had yet to be proven, and now as reality had closed in on me, I decided to face my new circumstances as a grown-up man.

Moments later, I hugged my family for the last time, and mother gave me chapati to take on board with me. I remember waving and waving and waving to my family, so much so that my wrist began to hurt as I held on tightly to my seat, despite the pounding of my heart. Beneath me, I could see the beautiful Lake Victoria, one of the world's largest fresh water lakes. I was mesmerized by my new circumstances. Everything around me was happening so fast that I wondered if I would ever catch up with the demands of this new chapter in my life. I was fascinated by the whole notion of flying and wished I had studied more about the Wright brothers and Emilia Earhart and her courageous flying adventures around the world.

Each passing minute aboard the Ethiopian Airlines Boeing 767 reminded me of the realization of my dream. I was leaving home for a year; I knew my departure was not in vain. It was rather a major blessing for me, my family, my community and most of all my country. Those thoughts helped to calm me down. I also knew that I was shouldering an immense responsibility. Out of 10 million Ugandans, I had been chosen to study abroad. Thinking about the whole situation helped me to put everything into perspective. But at the same time the weight of it rested on my little shoulders and seemed to push me deeper into the airplane seat. Yes, it would be very challenging to learn computer-aided woodworking in an all new Italian language. I was determined more than ever to excel.

By now, I had been studying English for a good twelve years, and on many occasions, I still felt incompetent despite my desire to master it. In retrospect, learning English had come with some tough sacrifices. My elementary school teacher, Mrs. Babukiza's approach had worked. She would have us memorize words, and have each of us recite them back. Our class was so small that if one of us failed reciting the word correctly, she would reach you with her cane. Some of my friends would try to hide, having gone through the same experience almost every day. But "evade and escape" did not seem to work too well with her cane that almost covered the entire breadth and width of the class. From my personal experience, I had mastered the technique of walking off that pain, but because we didn't have the freedom to move around, that pain seemed to shoot through your body like a bolt of lightning. On many occasions I would grit my teeth hoping to contain the pain and resist it like a tough man, but it cut deeply through my entire body like a brand new razor. That was extremely painful. However, living under that intense fear had motivated me to learn fast, and perhaps with those experiences subtracted from my life, I wouldn't be on the plane now. This experience, of course, was behind me now, although it was still vivid in my mind. I wondered if the Italian language teachers would as well impose this sort of intense disciplinary measure upon us.

About an hour through the flight, the stewardesses started serving dinner to the passengers. They were beautiful women dressed elegantly in their uniforms, something I had only seen on TV or in magazines. This really caught the best of my attention. As they approached our aisle, I wondered whether I should accept the meal and the cold drinks they were serving. My hesitation stemmed from my fear of not being able to afford the food.

"What would you like for dinner, Mr. Musaalo?" she asked. No one had ever addressed me as "Mr." before and this made me uncomfortable. I'd made up my mind not to eat food I had no money to pay for, so I answered I would pass. She appeared profoundly astonished that I had declined to eat and hesitated in her reaction. With a puzzled look, she went about her business. A few minutes later, I pulled out my home-cooked chapati meal, and started eating. Mother's chapatis were always the best, and I knew this would indeed be my last shot at Mother's home-style cooking.

My cousin who worked at the airport had given me twenty pounds to be used only when it was absolutely necessary. This money meant a lot to me—more than any other money anyone had ever given me. If I lost it, my life would be a disaster, especially in Rome, one of the world's most populous cities. After eight long hours, we started our decent to the Leonardo Da Vinci Airport, Italy's biggest airport. It was rather late in the evening when we started deplaning. I reached for my small bag and found my passport. Nervously, I walked down the aisles, of course with mixed emotions. The mere thought of thinking that I was now in Rome was exciting, but underneath this ecstatic moment, was my unsubdued fear of the new European world.

Rome, or Roma, occupies a treasured part in my heart. It was the first Metropolis I ever visited away from home. Cigarette smoke filled the air and I'd never seen so many people smoking at the same time. I often wondered if it was a hobby. How many people did it take to sweep the cigarette butts off the narrow streets? I wondered if the city would still be lit if they had a blackout. Even though I was later to live in Rimini for a longer period than I did in Rome, I always considered Rome as a home where I had no specific house, and Rimini as a place where I had a house and no home. It was the first European city I saw, and I adopted it as my second home. Rimini is a city in the Emilia-Romagna region of Italy. It is located on the Adriatic Sea, and probably the most famous seaside resort on the Adriatic Riviera.

When we left the embassy in Uganda, we were instructed to go straight to the *Ministero Degli Affari Esteri*, the Ministry of Foreign Affairs, upon our arrival. However, we landed in Rome after the office had closed and I had to quickly find a place to stay for the night. Rome is a beautiful city, and for someone raised within the outskirts of Kampala, a third world capital city, there were indeed many eye-opening things in my new surroundings that caught my attention. Life in Rome seemed exhilarating and somewhat precarious. The narrow streets were crowded with the tiniest cars I'd ever seen, the Cinquecento, Fiat's smallest model. They seemed to go in every direction without regard to traffic laws, like huge swarm of ants. One had to be very careful when stepping into the streets. Many angry drivers and pedestrians would shout and wave hand gestures, portraying their dismay at one another. On the opposite side of the street, I could see some couples staggering as they tried to make their way up the narrow lane. It was obvious that they were under some type of influence, and as I passed by the place where I had seen them standing, I caught sight of a pile of freshly used syringes, still dripping with some blood.

Nevertheless, Rome's atmosphere was alive, and its spirit adventurous. The people in Rome appeared to be resourceful. The roads were paved, and although they were the antithesis of immaculate, they were devoid of potholes. Rome was desperately overcrowded, both by people and cats. Every square foot was occupied by tall and short mediaeval buildings.

Roaming up and down the streets of Rome in desperation of catching a bus to head home were large groups of people from all walks of life, ranging from teenage students to older city dwellers. They were mostly Caucasian, although every so often some Asians and black folks would briskly walk by. Almost all the black folks acknowledged my presence by either smiling, waving or nodding their heads. I enthusiastically reciprocated the friendly gesture. Although I was not related to them, there was a strong bond between us. With this almost-assured social interaction, I should have interrupted them and asked for directions, but knowing that I was both linguistically handicapped and too scared to even try, I gave up that idea, a mistake that I regret up to today.

By now, darkness was closing in and most of the buildings were closing down, with the exception of Kiosks that continued to serve coffee (espresso) and sandwiches. In the meantime, I was getting hungry and cold. Should I stop someone now? I quietly debated in my heart. I knew that my dilemma and trepidation were exponentially increasing by the minute, and that if I were to find help, I had to act immediately. Perhaps as a result of all this unfamiliarity, I yearned for some simple empathy that mother had bestowed upon me while going through a hard day. But realizing quickly that neither family nor friends were with me, I came up with some quick alternatives.

The first alternative that I had in mind was to seek the assistance of the police, but as I looked around there were none to be found. Then I thought about finding a cheap hotel or *pensione*. I gathered myself again and presumptuously asked an Italian man, in English, whether he knew of any available hotels in the vicinity. He spoke English quite well to my astonishment, and he told me that late as it was, it would be impossible for me to find any free room. "Hotels in Rome are reserved during the day, and unless you know somebody, finding lodging in the evenings is virtually impossible." The man's comments intensified my worries. I do not recall very much what happened. But I knew I was running out of time. By this time I had been roaming the streets for a good five hours. I was very tired and hungry. The old saying that goes, "Rome was not built in a day," now made sense. I was learning this old saying the hard way. Gradually I started feeling dizzy and that's the last thing I felt before passing out.

I woke up the following morning only to find myself in a hospital, in my own cubicle. Puzzled, and terrified, I wondered whether my new circumstances were a dream. But realizing there were nurses racing back and forth from cubicle to cubicle to attend to some ill patients was enough evidence to ease my earlier doubts about this odd situation. "How did I get here and what had happened to me?" I wondered, knowing I had not come here out of the blue. I was coherent, with no restraints, and no part of my body hurt. I knew I was safe. Soon afterwards, a doctor who commanded a good knowledge of the English language told me around midnight some bypassers on one of the streets adjacent to the hospital had seen me fall, and they had called the hospital to inform them of my condition. Because I had a very shallow understanding of Italian then, I was unable to probe into what exactly had happened. But those kind men who alerted the hospital about my passing out will always occupy a special place in my heart because of their unwavering resolve to give me another shot at life. I convalesced quite quickly. I was still strong and coherent. Prior to being discharged from the hospital, the nurses handed me my worldly belongings, and directions to the Ministry of Foreign Affairs, which was just two blocks down the street. Within a few minutes, I arrived at the offices where a middle-aged short Italian man who had been awaiting my arrival, smilingly, ushered me into his office. His kind smile seemed to put me at ease and made me feel I was safe. As I sat down and put everything into perspective, a scripture in the Book of Matthew came to mind "Whatsoever you do unto the least of these my brothers, that you do unto me." I promised

God that from now on, I would always emulate this outstanding principle towards fellow men and women who were in dire need of my assistance.

I was one of 40 other students who had been granted the SCM fellowship to study for ten months in Rimini, Italy. Established in 1952, SCM is the leading producer of the most technologically advanced woodworking machines and systems. I discovered this information from the man who interviewed me. As I walked out of the door, I caught sight of two other new arrivals, waiting for their turns to be interviewed. Although I did not know where they hailed from, I was comforted to know that come departure time, there would be a few of us setting out to Rimini, our final destination. My two friends, as I was to soon learn, were from Bolivia, and as I reached out to help one of them carry his heavy suitcase, he quickly introduced himself to me as José and I quickly introduced myself with a firm handshake as Vincent from Uganda. We both smiled, for that's all we could do to express our acquaintance with one another. He later pulled out his train ticket and pointed to the city where we were going. I affirmatively shook my head in acknowledgment, and from then on, I realized I had just created a new friendship.

José was about forty years old; twice as old as the rest of us, and by virtue of his physical features one could quickly tell that he had spent a considerable amount of his life working hard. His fingers and hands were replete with calluses, the true vestige of an industrious man. I could relate to him very well. Two hours later, we all grabbed our possessions and followed José, who had been selected to be our interim leader. Because of the similarity between Spanish and Italian, José understood the language and directions better than the rest of us, and was able to translate for the group. He led us to a bus station where we boarded a bus and headed towards the center of the city. Once again, downtown Rome was inundated with heavy traffic. From my seat I could see angry, obnoxious drivers shouting at one another. Some were even out of their vehicles, pointing fingers at each other and shouting to the top of their voices. Only then did I come to the conclusion that even the Western world was not immune to the persistent commotion of the city.

In my first, short, and somewhat tumultuous experience in Rome, I learned more about poverty than I did in all my childhood days in Uganda. Beggars who were of Gypsy decent with their destitute families were persistently hustling bypassers for money. I'd never seen money beggars in such a humongous group before. Young teenage mothers using their desperate looking infants, some newly born, and others close to two years old, to solicit money. That was jaw-dropping. Churches adorned virtually every street, and in the Piazzas one could see the beautiful sculptures of baby Jesus and Mary. Almost everywhere I looked, I saw nuns and Catholic priests, and wondered how many of them resided here.

It was about 11:30 a.m. when we arrived at Rome's Termini railway station, the biggest and most congested railway station in Italy. As soon as the bus stopped, I reached out to give a hand to my friend José who appeared to be struggling with his baggage. *"Permesso, permesso,"* uttered a lady behind me, as she made her presence known. Not knowing what she meant, I fidgeted around and stepped back as she agitatedly jumped the baggage and mumbled a multitude of words. I could tell she was bothered by my apathetic attitude, but not knowing what she was saying, I was unable to react to her request. Months later, I discovered with deep regret that *permesso* was Italian for giving way to someone who was in a hurry, and that I'd breached that courtesy. José in the meantime beckoned us to follow him, and relying on his limited but better than our skills in Italian, we tagged along in single file until we arrived at the platform where we were supposed to catch the train in a couple of minutes. Behind us was a young male guitar player in a black leather jacket entertaining the waiting passengers whose songs seemed to catch the attention of the bypassers. Right next to him was a black hat turned upside down in which the reverent spectators, in appreciation, threw paper bills or coins at the end of every song. The songs had a sad appeal to them, and as I looked around I saw some folks shedding tears. Others were deeply meditating. Whatever the songs meant, they helped to console me and comfort me. Aside from boosting my morale, they helped me look forward to the future and lessen many of the worries I had carried since leaving my home.

Finally the train arrived and the anxious passengers started boarding. José, the good Samaritan, led us to a gorgeous compartment. Having put our bags in the small storage units above our seats, we sat down and looked forward to embarking on our journey. A few minutes later, we left Termini. Our departure was symbolic of a new life, fraught with multiple unknowns. However, those concerns were tempered by the excitement and gratitude I felt for what was to come. I recalled some of the events that had occurred in the past month. As I look back today, I see how miraculous and yes, intentional they were.

I was determined to stay awake as long as I could to view the beautiful scenery of rural Italy, but I fell short of this goal and within minutes I soon succumbed to sleep. I had not realized how the worry, excitement, anticipation, and physical effort had used up all my energy to the point where I could no longer fight off sleep. Several hours had passed when my friends woke me up to ask whether I was interested in buying a drink and sandwiches from the train waiter. Realizing that I had not yet exchanged my 20 British pounds for the Italian Lires, I passively declined the invitation. From my seat, I could see a few open fields with isolated herds of cows grazing in the beautiful meadows. Gorgeous fields of grass complemented the flat landscape, and although there were no farmers in the vicinity, my heart went out to them for the marvelous work they had done. "Maybe our farms back home would be this well maintained had we tractors and sprinkler systems," I thought to myself. I knew we could if the farmers had access to such advanced equipment. Gradually the sun started setting, and I had my first vision of the Italian sunset, as beautiful as any of the Italian masters could paint. Soon it was dark, and although by now the view from the train car was significantly limited, I enjoyed gazing at the well-lit cities and neighborhoods. It was all wondrous. Each vista that passed my window was one I had never seen or even imagined in my entire life. It was like opening a present every few minutes. At about 9 p.m., after several hours on a fast train, we arrived at Rimini.

Chapter 23

RIMINI AT NIGHT with its fancy antiquated buildings, cobblestone streets, sculptures, and billboards, resurrected my fantasies of a European city. Even though I was extremely tired, this breathtakingly beautiful scenery rejuvenated my body, and rekindled my admiration for the medieval towns. Surrounding me were groups of three to five Italians who had come to pick up their families and friends from the railway station. No one had come to meet us, and anxious to find the location of our hotel, José went to the information desk, where a lady picked up a small pamphlet entitled, *Tutto Citta* a title that I later learned meant "All City," and showed him where our hotel was and how to get there. Trusting and relying on José's sense of direction, we slowly walked out of the station to find a bus to take us to the hotel.

No sooner had I walked out of the railway station, than I was hit by a severe draft that penetrated my body from head to toe. Attempting to defend myself against this new and unusual attack on my body, I reached for my jacket, but it did not help much. Instead, my hands and toes were freezing. My eyes were watering, and my entire body was shivering. I could survive in 100+ degree hot temperatures in Uganda where the average low temperature is 62 degrees Fahrenheit, but my body had never experienced these freezing temperatures in this new world. This was the first of the many adjustment phases I would later endure.

It was now approaching 12:30 a.m., and besides us and a handful of hurrying pedestrians, there was no one on the cold streets, not even the beggars. The town was now temporarily deserted. José, who had just finished looking at the schedule, went around sharing what he had found out, I guess, relative to the bus services. He looked as if it was bad news.

Had the buses stopped for the night? And if indeed they had, what would be our fate? Would I freeze to death? Finally he approached me, and pointing to the schedule, he started mumbling some words I never understood. Realizing that there was absolutely no way a Ugandan could understand a Bolivian trying to explain an Italian bus schedule, I just nodded my head, showing interest in the message he was trying to explain. He then grabbed his suitcase, and beckoned us to follow him.

We started our trek like a platoon of soldiers, me also keeping an eye open for any polar bears that may be lurking in the darkened Italian alleyways. Because my body was frozen by now, I wondered how long it would take us to get to the hotel. About fifteen minutes later, two African students from Senegal stopped us, and after visiting with them led us to Hotel Nautic, located in Viserba, one of the many suburbs of Rimini.

I had never been to a hotel before that was this beautiful that was a three-star hotel. I had worked at Hotel Diplomate in Uganda but had never even imagined I would ever stay at one. This exotic upscale residence was magnificent and way beyond what I had expected. I had been told we would reside on one of the campuses owned by SCM in one of the dormitories, but not in such an upscale neighborhood.

Now the challenge ahead of me was to rise up to the occasion and adjust quickly to these lofty high standards. I had yearned for a better life, a life beyond farming, not because I dreaded it, but because I knew that if given the opportunity, I could make something out of my life. But on the other hand, with no tangible prospects or even opportunities ahead, I felt like I was building castles in the air. I had prayed fervently to God to make this possible and now here I was in the thick of these promises. God had finally sent down these promises like he sent manna to the Biblical Israelites to provide for them. This juxtaposition hit home, and if there had been a time in my life in which I had entertained any doubts about God's providence, this special moment had erased all my earlier doubts.

José rang the bell, and less than a minute later, a receptionist dressed in a colorful uniform ushered us in, to the immediate relief of my frozen body. He was a short plump man with a round face and a macho mustache, the kind that curls up at the ends. Nearby, I could see a team of bellboys rushing back and forth to pick up our luggage. No one had ever carried anything for me as part of their job before in my life. It was kind of embarrassing. As we walked into the hotel, the first things that caught my eye were the paintings that adorned the halls. These exquisite mediaeval paintings, which covered the walls from the ceiling down to the floor, seemed to add to the majestic and romantic atmosphere that surrounded me. I couldn't believe that I was basking in this beautiful picturesque scenery with chandeliers dancing above my head, and for a while it seemed like a fantasy world that I had sneaked into without permission.

This red-carpet-like treatment, at first, was beyond what I could handle, so much so, that I felt a little uncomfortable. "Only heads of states receive such a fancy reception," I thought. With a little bit of smile on my face, I decided that sometimes you just have to let nature take its course, and I would do my best to "endure" the attention directed at me. You have to enjoy what Heavenly Father blesses you with. Deep down in my heart I knew there were a lot of other people in my country who would've deserved being in my shoes much more than me. But I was convinced that God had chosen me for a reason that I couldn't understand at this time. Remembering that I was still this poor Ugandan lad who one time had walked on the dirt roads of

Kampala to go to school or run errands for my family was almost unbelievable. This feeling of humility tempered the feelings I had because of the opulent atmosphere and attention directed towards me by the hotel personnel.

In a grouchy voice, the receptionist, who I later learned was named Giuseppe shouted, *"Passaporti! Passaporti!"* and some additional words, which of course I couldn't grasp. I knew that passaporto was most likely a cognate word for "passport," so I immediately reached out and unzipped my bag to find it. By this time everybody had lined up, each holding a passport. Gazing ahead, I could see my colleagues filling out and signing some documents. Soon it was my turn, and raising his head, Giuseppe asked for my passport. He checked off my name on the list, filled out some information on the paper, and handed me a key to my room.

As I was making my way through this group of students, I noticed another South American student talking to the receptionist. Soon after that, the receptionist reached out and air-kissed the student on both cheeks. The student was visibly perplexed by what had just happened to him, and I will never forget his facial expression. His eyes popped out and he was as red as a tomato. What an interesting way of being introduced to the Italian culture, I thought. Before coming to Italy, I had been told that Italians are a passionate and loving people, though I had never expected that they would kiss a fellow man. Perhaps I should have learned how gestures, stances, and expressions communicate in the Italian culture. I should have found out which gestures are common to both cultures. Now I became aware that certain gestures did not always communicate the same cultural meaning. If only my friend had invested some time in explaining which gestures his culture had in common with the Italian culture, he could have felt comfortable in this awkward moment.

As I got to my room, I discovered that it was gorgeous, and, to crown it all, I had the entire room to myself. It was spacious and had the most comfortable bed. In addition, it had a bathroom, a television set, and even a balcony which opened up to a spectacular view of the Adriatic Sea. The lights reflected off the shores, and the waves, with the cool breeze, could be heard in the distance. Right off the beach I could see hundreds of big umbrellas left out on the beach in preparation for another exciting day at the sea. I surmised people would come during the day and swim some, then come back to sit comfortably under those umbrellas, protecting themselves from the surging heat. Others, hoping to get a tan, bathed in the warm rays of the sun.

At 8 a.m. the following morning we all went down for breakfast and we were introduced to the director of our school. He introduced himself to us both in English and Spanish and cordially welcomed us.

He was Tiberio, the director, a well-to-do Italian, what the Italians would call *L'uomo di Successo* or a "Man of Success." He was probably in his fifties, and very accomplished engineer in every sense of the word. He was distinguished and in the European style, his title always accompanied his name, probably because of the reputation and respect he had attained over the years in his profession. Our brief meeting with him ended with a short presentation of the SCM institute, its founder, its goals and its accomplishments. One of his assistants handed out a map that contained such information as the bus routes, and bus numbers, and the school location. With such vital and helpful information on my finger tips, I was ready to begin my challenging academic endeavors.

I woke up at 6 o'clock on Monday morning, and after breakfast, my new classmates and I walked to the bus stop. The fall term had just begun and large groups of Italian students were eagerly waiting for their respective buses to go to school. As the buses approached the bus stop, the students would rush for the door, hoping to find an empty seat. Finally our bus arrived and we boarded it with a lot of Italian students. Since there were no seats left, we stood in the aisle packed together with no room to breathe. This experience marked my first real introduction to the Italian language and its musicality. As the Italian students spoke to each other, they almost sounded as though they were singing, and from then on I always looked forward to hearing them speak every morning I stepped on the bus. Even though I didn't understand what was said in their conversations, I was gradually and surely becoming a fan of the language.

At about 8:30 we arrived at the institute, and as we walked through the building, we were again warmly received by our instructors who spoke a little English. We were separated into two groups, the students from South America with their own language teacher and those from the English-speaking countries with their teacher as well. It was comforting to know that I would be learning Italian through English, and this seemed to boost my confidence. Jumping into a new language without being introduced to it in a language that you understand can be frustrating.

The SCM institute was a technical school held in high regard by the Italian government and considered by many to be one of the best institutes in Europe. The school was designed partly to cater to the needs and education of the third world technicians and engineers. Following the three month study of the language, and hoping that by now we had mastered its basics, the course officially began. Most of my classes were trigonometry and designing, and so I spent most of my time drawing and designing models. Later on they introduced us to the computerized woodworking machines which we used to cut and shape the structures we had created during the first part of the course. We later used these pieces to make a finished product, such as a table, a chair, or a cabinet. We worked as teams, and I loved working with my colleagues from Pakistan, Nepal, India, Cameroon, Ethiopia, Peru, Bolivia, Ecuador, and Costa Rica. It felt as though we had our own miniature United Nations. In fact, we had several soccer matches amongst the continents. These matches were very competitive, and we hated to lose to the other continents. My friend Munga from Cameroon, our coach-player, would always say, "if you miss the ball, don't miss the leg," and that pep talk seemed to get everybody poised to win under all circumstances. This exciting moment made me relive the emotions of the World Cup.

Chapter 24

ESIRING TO BE fully involved in the religious affairs of the Italian culture, I continued to attend church services in Italian, even though I didn't understand the language. After all, I was a devout member of the Catholic Church. Prior to my departure, mother had encouraged me to hold on to the faith, especially while in Italy, the home of the Catholic Church—the Holy See. In fact, she naively believed that I would be able to have a one-on-one conversation with the Pope and that by shaking his hand, I would be the conduit through which all the blessings from the pontiff would be transmitted to both our home and family. Little did she know that her wishes were out of reach with reality. But, determined to console her, I bought her a holy rosary that was believed to have been blessed by the Pope.

One Sunday morning I was having breakfast as usual when José walked over to me and started talking to me, and as usual, I was having difficulty understanding what he was saying. Sensing that I couldn't grasp what he was saying, he reached out to his Spanish-Italian dictionary and pointed to the word *chiesa*. I quickly pulled out my Italian-English dictionary, looked up the word and discovered that it meant "church." I nodded my head, accompanied with a couple of gestures, trying to tell José that I was at that point in time waiting for my other classmates with whom I had regularly gone to church. But figuring that we all attended the same church, I agreed to join him anyway. As we proceeded down the street I quickly realized that we were headed to another stop, and as if that was not enough, it was a tram stop which we hardly ever used as a means of transportation. Not wanting to offend him, I boarded the tram and off we went. "Maybe we're going to another Catholic church," I wondered. Maybe José had somehow forgotten how to get to church. But, of course, I had no answers to those questions, and could only sit back and enjoy the ride. We finally got off the tram and began walking towards an office building across the street. It was right then that I realized this was not the same church, and I did not need anyone's help to figure this out. I knew there was no way out now so I put my curiosity and confusion aside and gracefully walked into the room.

I was surprised to see a congregation of about 30 people singing hymns in Italian. We must have been quite a spectacle, because I could see that we had diverted their attention. At that time I felt like returning to the hotel, but realizing that I had forgotten how we had arrived to the church was enough to dissuade me from even attempting to leave without José. And so I decided to stay, and soon found a seat in the pew with the faithful. Normally the Mass ceremony in the Catholic Church lasts 45 minutes. In this church as I realized, this was not the case. I was quickly getting bored! A few minutes later two young Caucasian men dressed in dark suites reverently walked in the room where we were congregated. They wore name tags, something I was not accustomed to seeing. I could tell they were lighter skinned compared to the Italians and I wondered if they were foreigners as well. When they walked over to me, I thought they were either the Police or part of the Immigration Personnel who tracked down undocumented foreigners.

Overcome by what could possibly happen to me, and well aware that I did not have my passport with me, I started fidgeting, and sweating in the process. My heart started beating even harder when they came and sat on either side of my seat. I started quickly rehearsing in broken Italian what I would have to tell them in case they inquired about my visa. A few days earlier the school director had repeatedly warned us about the dangers of leaving our passports at the hotel. No sooner had they sat down than they started asking me questions in Italian.

By now I was so terrified that my hair stood on end, and my blood ran cold. "This could be the end of my short lived stay in Italy," I thought. I tried to relax and calm myself down. Suddenly, the one closest to me started smiling at me as though he were gauging my demeanor. I smiled back, hoping that this reaction would mask my conspicuous fear and probably save my life. I do not know what these young men were thinking about me, but their genuine smiles made me feel at home with myself and even drove away all the fear within me. A couple of minutes later, I overheard them acknowledging in English the fact that I did not speak either Italian or French. My goodness, they speak English! They speak English! I silently took a deep breath, and with a sigh of relief, introduced myself as Vincent.

After the meeting, they asked me where I was from, and what I was doing in Italy. I told them that I was from Uganda, and that I was attending school in Rimini. They then proceeded to tell me that they were missionaries from the Church of Jesus Christ of Latter-day Saints, and that they had a message they wanted to share with me. It took me a little while to grasp what they were telling me. I had never spoken to a native English speaker, and I had such a hard time understanding them. They spoke a hundred times faster than any of my teachers in Uganda. When I finally settled down, I accepted their invitation to share their message with me on Monday evening.

It was now becoming apparent to me that José was somehow affiliated with this church either as a member or as a well-wisher. How would he have known of this church in such a short time of our stay in Italy? Maybe he was a member even before he arrived here. By this time, curiosity had taken its toll on me. A new church? English speaking missionaries? And what had compelled José to think I would be interested in any church other than the Catholic Church? I felt like I had turned my back on the Catholic Church. I was convinced I had made a major mistake by allowing the missionaries to visit me at the hotel.

Chapter 25

ONDAY CAME QUITE quickly and at six o'clock the missionaries arrived. We were still having dinner, so I invited
them to join us. They politely declined the invitation, but
instead chose to wait in the foyer. I did not want to keep them
waiting, so I ate as fast as I could. In the meantime José had spot-
ted the missionaries and was visiting with them. As soon as I
was through with my dinner, I led them to my room, and José
came along as well. The missionaries formally introduced themselves to me as Mormon missionaries from the United States.
"Missionaries from the United States? Why would they be preach-
ing the gospel in Italy, the headquarters of the Catholic church?
Aren't they in the wrong country? This does not make any sense
to me," I thought. "Mormons? Are they one of America's religious
sects?" Never in my life had I ever seriously pondered about
religion more than I did in these few seconds. There had been
certainly no need to. I had been raised in the Catholic Church,
and I was proud to be a Catholic. I had never been in the middle
of another religion.

"Before we go on" they continued, "Can we begin with a word
of prayer?"

"As you wish," I responded, not wanting to offend them.

I intently listened to one of them pray, and I heard him mention Christ's name. At this point I knew they believed in Christ.

Shortly after the prayer, they informed me that they had a message of Jesus Christ that they wanted to share with me. The Catholic Church teaches that the Holy Spirit abides where three people are gathered for a good cause, and sensing that this was an ideal moment, I consented to their request. Their message was in many ways a summation of what I had been taught in the Catholic church about Christ, until they showed me the Book of Mormon. To my surprise, it contained such ancient prophets as Nephi, Mosiah, and Alma that are not mentioned in the Bible.

Immediately chills started running through my body, and realizing that my curiosity was, at this point, becoming unbearable, I asked who these prophets were. Their response that Christ, in addition to ministering to the Israelites, had visited the inhabitants of the Americas shortly after His resurrection was overwhelming. I had learned of Christ through the Bible and through the gospel readings, but it had never occurred to me that He had preached the gospel to the ancient inhabitants of the Americas. True and accepted, I knew the United States was a super power. But it was almost impossible to swallow the authenticity of their story about Jesus Christ. Could it be possible that they were attempting to impose their version of Christ upon me? Then they showed me a filmstrip about a modern prophet named Joseph Smith. Again, this story, although interesting, made me more skeptical and more inquisitive than ever. Wasn't Pope John Paul II his chosen ecclesiastical leader? Why, then, did we need a modern prophet?

Towards the end of our meeting, they invited me to ask Heavenly Father if the message they had shared with me was true. As they bore their testimonies, I was overcome by a strong feeling of peace and comfort. They were very sincere. Their testimonies about Christ and his ministry on earth profoundly humbled me, and their positive perspective about life left an indelible mark on my heart. I needed friends, good friends that

I could count on, friends that I could trust, and I knew that God had sent these men to me for that very purpose. All of a sudden, my doubts seemed to subside, and the reason for my being in Italy began to take on a new meaning. There was a feeling of reassurance, and suddenly, the last pieces of the puzzle fell into place. Heavenly Father had orchestrated my coming to Italy and I had promised to learn of Him and develop more faith in Him. This was an opportunity for me to accomplish that goal. Even though the missionaries hadn't asked me to be baptized, I had strong feelings about changing my life and rechanneling it towards God who had done so much for me. For the first time my eyes were opened to a God that was very close to me, that I could talk to and interact with on a personal basis, as apposed to the Catholic way of having someone intercede in your behalf. Prior to meeting the missionaries, I believed that God was so distant.

A week later I was having breakfast when the hotel manager came over to my table and told me that someone wanted to talk to me on the phone. "Who could it be?" I wondered. I quickly ran to the phone and as soon as I answered it a lady who spoke English with a Ugandan accent informed me that I needed to go to Rome to meet with the then Ugandan Ambassador. Before she hung up the phone she requested that I bring my passport with me. Was there something wrong with my passport? Could it be that the Italian Government had requested that I be deported? It dawned on me at this time that the Ugandan lady had not given me the address to the Embassy in Rome. These thoughts seemed to penetrate my mind from all directions, and the more I tried to push them aside, the more they conquered my mind, so much so, that I lost all form of concentration for most of that day. After supper that evening, I retreated to my room and started preparing for what I considered the scariest journey of my life. "If I can hardly get myself around the hotel, how can I pull off this trip single-handedly," I thought to myself. When I couldn't find either consolation, or empathy from my newly acquired friends, for neither one of them envied my situation, I retired to bed. I woke up exhausted the following morning, had my usual breakfast, and set out to the bus stop.

History has a way of repeating itself, and I had noticed this pattern occur several times in my life. "Perhaps I will do well this time around," I pondered. After all, this would mark my second time in Rome. But then I realized that I did not have any control over any future events. The only way I could avoid any major catastrophes from happening to me was through trusting God. At 9:45 a.m. we took off in the "Espresso train," the fastest they have in Italy, bound for Roma. My compartment was comfortable, and Italians seated by me engaged me in several conversations, and to my surprise each time I mentioned I was from Uganda, they would inquire as to the whereabouts of Idi Amin, the tyrant. Although I was excited to report about his eviction from Uganda, it was discomforting to realize that all that the Italians knew about Uganda was through this repressive dictator who had orchestrated the massive killings of innocent civilians. On the contrary, I was impressed by how much they knew about international politics.

We arrived in Roma at about 4 o'clock, and as soon as I got off the train, I headed to the information booth, and using my dictionary, pointed to the word Embassy. "*Ambasciata?*"

"*Di dove sei?*"—"Where are you from?" I had just learned that phrase in our language class at the SCM institute, and I quickly responded, "Uganda." Pulling out a big directory, she directed me to a seat, and proceeded on with her search. In a couple of minutes, she returned and smilingly handed me the address scribbled on the paper, with directions to the Embassy. I bought a bus ticket and caught the next bus to the Ugandan Embassy.

I walked straight to the building and before I rang the bell, all my fear set in. I had never met people of such high caliber and dignity, and I was uncomfortable with the entire situation. A lady acknowledging my arrival inquired if I was "Mr. Musaalo." I was astonished by this title.

"Yes," I quickly responded. "Vincent Musaalo."

"Unfortunately you can't see the Ambassador today," she said. "Something came up. He is meeting with some Government officials. He will be available to see you tomorrow." Tomorrow? Where would I stay for the night? I didn't have enough money. All the money I had left was for my trip back home.

"Can I spend the night here?" I inquired.

"I'm afraid not," she replied. "We're not responsible for your lodging." I was shocked and dumbfounded. Where do I go from here? I quickly walked out of the embassy and caught the bus back to the termini station to hatch out some new ideas. "If the worse comes to the worst," I thought to myself, "I will spend the night at the station."

I walked around for a little while in desperation, wondering how I could overcome this moment that was fraught with despair. Almost all the seats were taken and people seemed to be stuck on them, as though they were sending a message across that they were here to stay, at least for the entire night. I thought about sleeping on the floor as a last resort, but then I realized that I didn't have any bedding. In the background, the police were at work waking up people who thought they had secured a night's resting place.

At that moment, for some reason, I reached for my wallet, and luckily I discovered a business card that the missionaries had given me prior to leaving the hotel. Skimming over it, I noticed that towards the bottom it said *Missione Italiana Di Roma* and underneath it was a telephone number. I had played all of my cards and this was my last shot; so I quickly bought some token money for the telephone. Looking around, I saw a long line of people in the distance, and there was a phone at the front of the line. I took my place at the end of the line and anxiously awaited my turn. Examining the token, I noticed that it had a line that ran across it. I wondered why it had been minted that way. Soon it was my turn. I attempted to put the coin through the slot, but to my disappointment, it wouldn't go in. I tried again, but to no avail. In the background I could hear people grumbling, wondering why it was taking me so long.

The pressure was on, and I could feel it pinching each part of my body. Realizing that I was holding up the entire line, I quickly surrendered and went back to the end, ready to make another attempt. Reaching the telephone a second time, I tried to push the coin through the slot. I knew there was a certain way it had to be aligned with the slot, but to my dismay, I couldn't figure it out. The grumbling began again, and I withdrew out of frustration. By this time I had been trying for over an hour and I was getting desperate. The line kept on getting longer and longer as the trains arrived at the station and as the impatient people desperately waited for their families to pick them up. I again took my place at the end of the line, knowing it would take me another twenty minutes to reach the telephone.

I was hoping against hopes that I would be successful this time around. As I faced the phone, I took a deep breath and slowly put the token up to the slot. Again it was rejected, but I had made up my mind to somehow make this a successful attempt. If this didn't work, I could be stranded here, and my life would be in jeopardy. Gathering myself up, I reassured myself that I could do it. I was determined to invest all my effort in what seemed to be an insurmountable problem. As I began to make the attempt, a white hand reached around from behind, gently took that token from my hand and carefully slid it into the slot. He made what had taken me hours to do look so simple. I was so embarrassed and ashamed of myself, so much so, that I was unable to turn around and look him in the eyes to thank him.

I made the phone call to the mission home. Someone answered the phone and asked if he could offer me any help. I explained who I was and my encounter with the missionaries affiliated with this church in Rimini. I then told him my predicament. Having listened to my situation, he offered two choices to me: he could give me some money to stay at a hotel, or I could go stay at his home for the night. Fearing the intricacies associated with finding a hotel at this late hour, I chose to spend the night at his home. He wholeheartedly gave me directions to the mission home, and looked forward to meeting me there.

As I hung up the phone and walked away from that endless line to the bus stop, I could not get my mind off of that wonderful man who, moments ago had come to my immediate rescue. It dawned on me at that moment that even the simplest of things can be the most challenging and that God always puts His hand in to carry us along, just as that man did for me that evening. That man saved my life.

Overcome by such indescribable joy, I bought a bus ticket and caught the next bus that took me all the way to the Mission Home. Upon my arrival there, I was met by a middle-aged man who introduced himself as President Williams, the Mission President. He was a jovial man, and you could immediately tell there was something special about him. He empathized with my situation and quickly invited me to join his family at the dinner table. I do not remember much of the conversation that night, except for the brief visit we had in which he shared with me the Gospel of Jesus Christ. I retired to bed with such a great understanding of Jesus Christ and what He meant for me in my life. I woke up early the following morning and had breakfast with the President's family. He wished me well and encouraged me to continue listening to the message that the missionaries had prepared for me. I boarded the bus with a lot of indebtedness to this man for taking me in as a stranger. I was eager to continue my relationship with him.

I soon arrived at the Embassy, and before I rang the bell, my fear again set in, hoping that this wouldn't be a déjà vu. The same lady acknowledged my arrival with "Mr. Musaalo, please take a seat," and then said, "The Ambassador is talking with someone on the phone, and as soon as he's done, I'll call him to tell him you're here." She soon returned with a few Ugandan newspapers, and invited me to help myself. It was exciting to read the local newspapers from home and, as usual, I flipped to the sports section to catch up on the local soccer news. No sooner had I put the paper down than the lady told me that the Ambassador was off the phone and was waiting for me. I briskly walked to his office and shook his hand.

"Well, Mr. Musaalo," he said. Not again, I thought. What is up with this 'Mister' thing? "We have been informed by the government that you are currently attending school in this country. By law, we require that you provide us with your passport number. In other words, we want you to be registered with the Ugandan Embassy here in Rome, and in case of any emergency, please contact us as soon as possible. We wanted to meet you in person, and that's why we had you come here." As soon as our meeting ended, I left the Embassy and headed to Rimini, my home away from home.

Chapter 26

RESUMED MEETING WITH the missionaries upon my return from Rome. Somehow, the Mission President had phoned the missionaries and relayed his encounter with me while in Rome. They told me he was excited about talking with me about the gospel while I was there and urged the missionaries to continue sharing the gospel discussions with me. I will never forget the excitement on their countenances as they invited me again to join them in discussing this new, and for some reason, enticingly familiar church. I was not the only one they were sharing the gospel with, and because of my outlook and openness, the missionaries always felt compelled to invite me to join them as they visited with the rest of the investigators at the church. This was always exciting because as I shared my feelings about Christ, I felt closer to Him. By the same token, I was enormously touched when the rest of the investigators shared their experiences and feelings about God and, of course, Jesus Christ. Looking back it was quite unusual. What prompted the missionaries to take me, a new investigator still with many unanswered questions, with them to teach others?

One day we were meeting in one of the church rooms discussing the purpose of life. I wondered why the conversation had shifted from the gospel in general to this topic. This abrupt change did not appear to make any sense. The questions sounded rhetorical. The purpose of life, I thought, is to go to school, find a job, raise a family and provide for their needs. That's what mother had taught me, and that's what everybody around me tried to accomplish in life. And considering what I had seen and experienced in Uganda, one might say firstly I was taught just to survive. This was the conventional wisdom that had guided me and motivated me to aspire for greater things in life. "I will ask you again," the missionary continued presumptuously, "what is the purpose of life?" One of the investigators stood up and said that the purpose of life is to provide for family and to make them happy. "That's a good answer," he replied, "but how does this happiness relate to God?"

It was at this point that the whole conversation started making sense to me. Almost as if I were struck by a bolt of lightning, I quickly came to the realization that the ultimate purpose of this life was to be in harmony with God's commandments. I was about to raise my hand and express my feelings, when the missionary said, "The purpose of this life is to meet God." These words indeed hit home for a couple of reasons. If indeed God had paved my way and provided me with all the blessings of life, such as my family, my friends, my life, it was evident that by all the events in my life—He loved me. And so, in order for me to show my indebtedness to Him, I had to learn of Him, to emulate His Son and to serve those around me as His loyal disciple.

I accepted to be baptized as a member of Christ's church on the 6th of December 1987, because I was convinced beyond any reasonable doubt that God wanted me to be part of it. The day I made my decision to be baptized is very special in my life and I remember that the world around me seemed to be at peace. I was overcome by such a profound feeling of vitality and confidence and, most of all, a love for humanity. Life was worth living and everything fell into place and made sense. I could see now the unfolding of a new chapter in my life. The hand of God in the events of my life was now becoming clear. Where I was born, to whom I was born, the experiences, good and bad, of my youth. Walking into the Italian Embassy, running into the woman at the embassy and amazingly finding myself in Italy. And now, by some miracle, being granted the greatest of all gifts, the knowledge of my purpose on earth and my relationship with my God. Now I realized that meeting José was not just a coincidence, but that God had placed him in my path for a reason. He wanted me to know about him and His church. And the path which led me to that point, however miraculous or amazing at first look, was devised by my Father in Heaven for His purpose. What I had first thought happened because of "luck, fate" or "fortune" happened because of LOVE. His love for me, preparing me and guiding me on this fantastic journey towards Him. Who would have imagined that a devout Catholic from Uganda would learn of the Latter-day Saint Church through a Latter-day Saint from Bolivia in Italy?

Noticing that I still had a long way to go with the language, the missionaries dedicated part of their time towards teaching me Italian. Following each visit, they would conjugate a verb or two in Italian and have me practice forming sentences with them. I complemented these weekly Italian lessons with participation in the Sunday school gospel discussions. Only two members out of forty spoke English, and, in order for me to make myself acquainted and build a relationship of trust, I had to learn to speak Italian. In fact, I was invited on many occasions to dine with the members. Usually, as I would knock on the door or ring the doorbell, their children would run to see who it was. Before opening the door, they would look through the peephole and yell back to their mothers, "It is the African man who does not speak Italian very well!" That became my nickname for the first five months of my stay in that area. Little children are always candid about things, and these kids were no exception. They always corrected me. Their parents wouldn't, perhaps in fear of offending me.

In the mean time, my friendship with José, that kind man who was so instrumental in changing my life, grew by leaps and bounds. Now I could talk to him with ease, a miracle that we probably had not anticipated on happening this soon, but which we both witnessed. José told me that he had met the church through missionaries in La Paz, Bolivia, the home of the Andes Mountains. He was a South American Indian who had overcome the shackles of poverty through hard work and sacrifice to later become a head technician for a big industry in La Paz. "I couldn't have gotten where I am without God," I remember him reiterating these words with such a great deal of conviction and optimism. I did not know much about Bolivia then, but I could only imagine how hard it must have been for him. Now I finally understood why he was so eager to share this message with me.

Chapter 27

NOTHING ACCELERATED MY learning of the Italian language as much as the free language lessons I received from both the missionaries and the members of the church. My interaction with them significantly helped me to develop both my communication and social skills. By now, I had learned Italian very well. I could participate in conversations, haggle at the open markets, and buy groceries at the supermarket. But even more exciting, I now understood all my classes that were offered in Italian at the SCM institute. Sometimes I volunteered at the institute, assisting some of my colleagues who were still struggling.

What made school more exciting were the monthly countryside trips which the Institute organized for us to visit the most outstanding wood-processing plants in Italy. These trips, although heavily educational, often led us to some of the most popular destinations in Italy such as Rome, Florence, Bologna, Milan, Venice, and Turin. There was always a lot to see, and we were exposed to Italy's diverse cultures. These trips introduced me to some of the world's most picturesque vistas. Standing in front of the classic work of Leonardo da Vinci and The Last Supper, and other breathtaking works of art in these historical cities left an indelible mark on my heart. Where I came from there was much natural beauty, but the evil that men did to my society sniffled that beauty which came from man and was freely expressed in art.

We completed our course in July of 1988, and I was ready to take an oral examination, Italy's famous *viva voce* style of testing. I was now 20 years of age and been a member of the church for eight months. Each one of us made an appearance before our teachers, who would proceed asking any question they deemed appropriate. We never knew what they would ask, and perhaps that explains why I was so stressed. I felt as nervous as I did as a young boy standing in front of my school's headmaster.

Soon it was my turn. I took a long breath and walked to the room. I was certainly relying on all I had learned about prayer in my church. I was so stressed, and neither one of the teachers was smiling. There were a few advanced industrial woodworking systems and system manuals scattered on the table, which I immediately recognized from class. On another table I could see different types of wood, one of which was mahogany, my favorite. The questions began. The first instructor asked me to name the different types of wood. I stammered a little, trying to remember the different types of wood I had memorized the night before. I could not remember, and my mind was blank. Then in about a minute or so, my mind was inundated with all the names. I quickly took a piece of paper and wrote as fast as I could. The instructor then looked at me and said you have two minutes left to give me the answer to the question. I looked at the displayed wood and rapidly matched them with the scientific names. I knew I had done fairly well, and I could see the instructor writing down some information. Then my laboratory instructor asked me to name the parts of one of the machines, and explain how it worked. Naming the part of the machine was not a problem, for I knew how each part worked, but I could not explain in Italian how it worked. I would start, stop, and start over again, but I just couldn't fully answer the question. He had a replica of the machine and asked me to demonstrate to the instructors how it functioned. I grabbed a piece of chalk and proceeded, while answering questions along the way. These tests lasted two days, and on the 28th of July 1988, I received a diploma in woodworking technology from the SCM institute. We hugged and cheered each other as each of our names were announced. The ceremony was so colorful, and we celebrated it in the Italian fashion. There was so much to eat, and so much to drink for those who love Italian wine.

Chapter 28

THE ROAD WAS deserted when I stepped out of my hotel room, and headed to the balcony overlooking the Adriatic Sea. I had religiously come to this spot every evening to catch the breathtakingly gorgeous sunsets. The skies were flooded with flocks of chirping birds which seemed to be migrating to the only destination they knew, a new place that would provide them a temporary abode. I was homesick knowing that within a fortnight school in Rimini, Italy would be over, and that I would be leaving my new western life behind to return to my native Uganda.

My new friends, the American missionaries, who had baptized me, were sad I would be relocating shortly, but were also overjoyed to know I would be sharing the gospel with my friends and relatives at home. I knew that if this was God's new work for me, then He would provide the courage and words. I was looking forward to sharing the message that Heavenly Father knows the details of our lives.

Of course, I couldn't wait to see mother again. But most of all, I couldn't wait to console her, to reminisce Francis' life, and the last moments she had spent with him. I had received a letter from him several months earlier in which he had expressed his afflictions with asthma. Shortly thereafter, his health deteriorated, and he passed away. His passing demoralized me more than I can express. Not being able to attend his burial remains something I will never completely reconcile.

Despite the sad news, my country was starting to witness some glimmer of hope. The state imposed curfews had been gradually lifted, and Ugandans, after so many years, were free from the whizzing bullets that had since been ubiquitous. People were slowly working their way from hurt and betrayal, and the key to healing turned out to be the same for each person. Each had a hurt he had to forgive; the neighbor who had conspired against him, the pseudo-friend who had reported him to the State Research Bureau, and the sadistic opportunist who had lost his soul to gain the short-lived popularity in a totalitarian regime. In their own time and in their own way, people worked through the deep pain within them. The old adage, "To understand all is to forgive all," seemed to make sense. Uganda was now a country where all those who had lost their loved ones, those like my high school history teacher, Baguma, who had lost a limb to a grenade during the civil war, and those whose lives had been adversely affected in unfathomable ways, could learn to live again, unafraid, in the beautiful country that Sir Winston Churchill knew as the pearl of Africa.

Chapter 29

A S I CONTINUED to grow in my life and in the gospel, it became clear to me how involved God is in the events of our lives. They say a sparrow does not fall without the Father knowing about it. At the time of the events of my youth in Uganda, I would have considered myself of no more importance than one little sparrow. But now I know He was there throughout each struggle in my life; when I hid under the bed from the militia, running from gunfire, and even learning of my father's murder. He led and guided me step by step to where he wanted me to be and prepared and inspired others to assist along the way; an embassy lady, the man with a quiet hand who helped me insert the coin into the phone slot at the train station, an airline attendant with a kind face, a charitable Mission President, a kind branch president, Ezio Caramia, who warmly welcomed me to church each Sunday, and especially my brother, José. José, who, even not being able to communicate with me, knew he was to invite me to church for an important reason, a reason which has had eternal results.

After completing school, I was able to serve for two years as a missionary in Italy myself. While serving in that capacity, I met Glenna Smith, a fellow missionary in Italy, whose family kindly funded my formal education at Brigham Young University. I was also wonderfully blessed while attending the university to find the woman who became my wife and mother of my children.

I eventually was able to teach Italian to missionaries at the Missionary Training Center for five years, and work for that same church that was brought so miraculously to me.

We are not just mere pinballs randomly bouncing off this and that and going where chance or fate leads us. But a loving Father in Heaven leads us and guides us as an earthly father would. As great as His influence was in my early life, absent the little effort on my part to seek it out, I have since learned I can go to Him and ask for specific guidance and inspiration regarding the choices and decisions I have to make every day as an employee, husband and father. I know there is not one plan of salvation but as many plans as there are his children who come to earth. He is still there every day, as much as he was in Uganda and in Italy. His still small voice still speaks to his son.

Made in the USA
Columbia, SC
19 October 2017